T0211625

Communications
in Computer and Information Science   1433

More information about this series at http://www.springer.com/series/7899

María J. Abásolo · Jorge Abreu ·
Pedro Almeida · Telmo Silva (Eds.)

Applications and Usability of Interactive TV

9th Iberoamerican Conference, jAUTI 2020
Aveiro, Portugal, December 18, 2020
Revised Selected Papers

 Springer

Editors
María J. Abásolo 🆔
National University of La Plata
La Plata, Argentina

Jorge Abreu
University of Aveiro
Aveiro, Portugal

Pedro Almeida
University of Aveiro
Aveiro, Portugal

Telmo Silva 🆔
University of Aveiro
Aveiro, Portugal

ISSN 1865-0929   ISSN 1865-0937 (electronic)
Communications in Computer and Information Science
ISBN 978-3-030-81995-8   ISBN 978-3-030-81996-5 (eBook)
https://doi.org/10.1007/978-3-030-81996-5

This Springer imprint is published by the registered company Springer Nature Switzerland AG
The registered company address is: Gewerbestrasse 11, 6330 Cham, Switzerland

Preface

The 9th Iberoamerican Conference on Applications and Usability of Interactive TV (jAUTI 2020) was organized by the Social iTV group of the DigiMedia Research Unit of the University of Aveiro (Aveiro, Portugal) in conjunction with RedAUTI (Thematic Network on Applications and Usability of Interactive Digital Television). RedAUTI consists of 32 research groups from universities in 13 Ibero-American countries (Argentina, Brazil, Colombia, Costa Rica, Cuba, Chile, Ecuador, Spain, Guatemala, Peru, Portugal, Uruguay, and Venezuela).

This year's edition was held on December 18, 2020, in an online meeting due to the context of the COVID-19 pandemic, which did not prevent the participation of researchers from various universities (specifically from Europe and America) and from industry from sharing their research work.

These proceedings contain a collection of 12 papers referring to the design, development, and user experiences of applications for Interactive Digital Television and related technologies, selected from the 35 papers accepted at the event after a peer-review process, that was later extended and underwent a second peer-review process.

December 2020

María J. Abásolo
Jorge Abreu
Pedro Almeida
Telmo Silva

Organization

Program Chairs

María J. Abásolo	National University of La Plata, Argentina
Jorge Abreu	University of Aveiro, Portugal
Pedro Almeida	University of Aveiro, Portugal
Telmo Silva	University of Aveiro, Portugal

Program Committee

Jose Luis Arciniegas Herrera	University of Cauca, Colombia
Hernán Astudillo	Technical University Federico Santa María, Chile
Sandra Baldassarri	University of Zaragoza, Spain
Valdecir Becker	Federal University of Paraíba, Brazil
Vagner Beserra	Universidad of Tarapacá, Chile
Pedro Beça	University of Aveiro
José María Buades Rubio	University of the Balearic Islands, Spain
Bernardo Cardoso	University of Aveiro, Portugal
Sandra Casas	National University of Southern Patagonia, Argentina
Fernanda Chocron Miranda	Federal University of Pará, Brazil
Cesar Collazos	University of Cauca, Colombia
Armando De Giusti	National University of La Plata, Argentina
Daniel Gambaro	University Anhembi Morumbi, Brazil
Angel García Crespo	University Carlos III of Madrid, Spain
Israel González Carrasco	University Carlos III of Madrid, Spain
Manuel González Hidalgo	University of the Balearic Islands, Spain
Roberto Guerrero	National University of San Luis, Argentina
Raphael Irerê	UniProjeção, Brazil
Anelise Jantsch	Federal University of Rio Grande do Sul, Brazil
Cristina Manresa Yee	University of the Balearic Islands, Spain
Oscar Mealha	University of Aveiro, Portugal
Francisco Montero	University of Castilla-La Mancha, Spain
Patrícia Oliveira	University of Aveiro, Portugal
Rita Oliveira	University of Aveiro, Portugal
Antoni Oliver	University of the Balearic Islands, Spain
Gonzalo Olmedo	University of the Armed Forces, Ecuador
Emili Pico	Autonomous University of Barcelona, Spain
Joaquín Pina Amargós	Technological University of Havana "José Antonio Echeverría", Cuba
Alcina Maria Prata	Polytechnic Institute of Setúbal, Portugal
Tânia Ribeiro	University of Aveiro, Portugal

Miguel Angel Rodrigo Alonso	University of Córdoba, Spain
Josemar Rodrigues de Souza	University of Bahia State, Brazil
Gustavo Rossi	National University of La Plata, Argentina
Beatriz Sainz de Abajo	University of Valladolid, Spain
Rita Santos	University of Aveiro, Portugal
Raisa Socorro Llanes	Technological University of Havana "José Antonio Echeverría", Cuba
Ana Velhinho	University of Aveiro, Portugal

Contents

iTV for the Elderly

Usability and UX Evaluations

Audiovisual Content and Experiences

Sharing and Visualizing Collective Memories – Contexts and Strategies for a Participatory Platform

Ana Velhinho[(⊠)] [iD] and Pedro Almeida [iD]

Digimedia, Department of Communication and Arts, University of Aveiro, Aveiro, Portugal
{ana.velhinho,almeida}@ua.com

Abstract. Technology can be designed to strengthen the participatory culture and giving a voice to people through User-Generated Content (UGC). Such practices may also influence the way we engage with places and communities. In this regard, we propose the conceptualization of an online platform to promote participation and preserve audiovisual records of shared experiences. Memories attached to places and cultural events, such as concerts, traditional celebrations and visits to landmarks and exhibitions, are frequently captured on multimedia records, which are often shared online by those who experienced them. The aggregation and correlation of these audiovisual resources, in a participatory platform, may enhance these experiences through forms of presentation based on multiple perspectives, making them collective. To gather insights and make proof of concept the method of exploratory interviews followed by a qualitative content analysis was adopted. Hence, the conceptualization of a digital platform that allows the creation of a living collaborative archive that preserves the uniqueness of each resource, but, in addition, allows an overview and combination of other participants' contributions, was presented to experts within the areas of archives, museology, heritage, ethnography, community projects, cultural events, design, participatory media and digital platforms. This paper presents a segment of the interviews' results concerning relevant use contexts along with recommendation and strategies for collection, visualization and participation to guide the development process of prototypes to be tested with target-users, whining a PhD research.

Keywords: Collective memory · Participatory platform · Experts · Interviews

1 Introduction

This paper aims to present the qualitative results gathered with experts about the concept of a participatory platform to share and visualize audiovisual collective memories, within a PhD research about the role of participation in the 21st century visual culture. In terms of structure, the document comprises six sections: the introduction to the study; the contextualization of the main concepts and authors in terms of theoretical background and related work; the outline of the main goals of the platform and the overall concept; the methodology and objectives of the paper; the presentation of results regarding use contexts and strategies; the discussion of results, opportunities and challenges and; the overview of contributions for future work.

© Springer Nature Switzerland AG 2021
M. J. Abásolo et al. (Eds.): jAUTI 2020, CCIS 1433, pp. 3–14, 2021.
https://doi.org/10.1007/978-3-030-81996-5_1

2 Theoretical Background and Related Work

2.1 User Participation and Digital Storytelling

The increasing possibilities for online participation, by means of User Generated Content (UGC) and life testimonials, are gradually being regarded as relevant contributions for, among others, building collective memories and encouraging user-led practices to safeguard communal legacies [1]. Paved by a *convergence culture* [2], participatory media contribute to build a sense of community, as people actively create and share content around common interests. Participation through UGC enables user control but, at the same time, opens new possibilities for visual presentation, since the same data can be tailored to tell different stories using distinct visualization models and aiming to achieve richer and more compelling stories [3]. Additionally, mobile became a trend as a medium-specific genre, giving rise to many formats based on the coaction between visual codes, narrative, and technical possibilities [4].

Currently, content production uses the affordances of Web 2.0 and mashup technologies [5] to deliver media that combine human and software agency to increase value when exploring physical places. Geolocation services, like Google Maps and other applications based on the individual and community displacements, have mainstreamed digital mapping as a daily practice, applied to tourism, education, gaming and utility services. Locative technologies can be boosters of place-based storytelling and promote real-time awareness, enhancing experiences by triggering contextual information. These mediated geographies can be created by a *collective intelligence* [6], using networks of users that structure and expand meaning within existing information. In this regard, participatory platforms can promote social dynamics around media and operate as means of expression and cohesion for different groups, while also contributing to generate and expand communal archives.

Approaching events as shared constructs amplifies how experiences are enjoyed when they occur, and also motivates keeping records for the future. These digital records (photos, videos, comments) are embedded with emotional value that surpasses their documental role. That is why many social media applications, like Facebook, Instagram or Google Photos, increasingly explore the sense of nostalgia, by sending notifications about past publications to celebrate memories. Such strategies induce the feeling of reliving the moments and the sense of belonging to a community, motivating social engagement. These interactions tend to rely on UGC, which is remixed and replicated to convey group storytelling [7] thus becoming more relatable.

2.2 Visualization Models Applied to Human Computer Interaction (HCI)

Considering the importance of visualization in the concept of the proposed platform is important to consider reference authors in the field of Information Design, such as Edward Tufte, known for detailing principles and models for coding and envisioning information into manageable knowledge [8, 9]. Also, relevant to be mentioned is the subfield of Information Visualization (InfoVis), which was adopted in the field of HCI to describe systems that usually rely on interactive graphics. In this context, Ben Shneiderman [10] introduced the mantra of visualization – "Overview first, zoom and filter, then details on-demand" – that highpoints the importance of maintaining a sense of context and control over the information to identify and deepen the users' interests. Another important aspect regarding means of attaching emotion to visualization is storytelling, approached by the genre of *narrative visualization* coined by Segel and Heer [3]. Also, the emergence of visualizations with larger data sets has promoted the update of taxonomies [11] to accommodate cutting-edge examples instigated by creative tools. Considering the diversity of genres and purposes, is important to distinguish two major types of visualizations: one that is explanatory and therefore task-oriented; and other that is exploratory, inviting to a contemplative and playful fruition, usually called *casual visualizations* [12], which includes artistic and participatory approaches. To inform the ideation process of the proposed platform the models and principles of the aforementioned reference authors were considered along with a selection of state-of-the-art projects exploring casual visualizations that correlate resources. The projects were distributed in two groups (see Fig. 1): 1) institutional websites and commercial apps inspired by social platforms; 2) artistic and research projects with experimental visualization approaches.

Fig. 1. Groups of selected related work: websites and apps (http://www.museudapessoa.net/pt/home; https://www.historypin.org/en/; https://www.polarsteps.com/; https://www.sturevents.com/) and; artistic and R&D projects (http://www.field-works.net/; Meireles, [11], p. 42; http://intuitionanalytics.com/other/lostalgic/; http://on-broadway.nyc/).

3   The Concept of the Platform

The main goal of the proposed platform is to give autonomy to users to collect and share UGC of collective experiences to create richer narratives based on correlated visualizations (combining, for example, time, geolocation, semantic correlation, networks of users, etc.) aiming to preserve the uniqueness of each resource. It is also aimed to provide an overview of the other participants' contributions to build an expanded and living archive. The proposed concept was subjected to a first stage of evaluation by means of a video presentation to a group of experts (see Fig. 2) followed by a semi-structured interview. The concept was briefly explained with a voiceover: "(1) *Imagine a mobile app that allows you to share records of past or ongoing events with people who have also been there or have relevant information about them... / (2)... to obtain visualizations that combine resources from multiple users boosted by social engagement and the creation of new connections between content, to enhance the depiction and get a deeper understanding of the event. As a collaborative living archive, this system aims to generate forms of visualization that are modelled according to users' participation... / (3)... and also to generate 'snapshots' that synthesize and evoke the collective memory of that event, which can be saved and shared with others*".

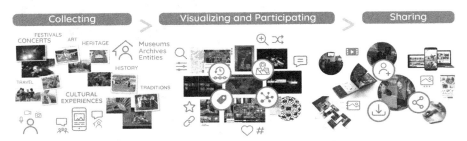

Fig. 2. Screenshots of animated infographics included in the video of the platform concept.

4   Methodology

The current research adopts a Grounded Theory methodology [13] with a Participatory Design approach [14] relying on mixed methods. This paper presents the qualitative data gathered from exploratory interviews with experts towards the systematization of guidelines to the prototype development of a participatory platform for easy collection and correlated semantic presentation of audiovisual records of collective experiences. The identification of a set of visualization models and review of related projects led to the ideation of the platform concept that was presented to a group of experts to gather qualitative insights through semi-structured interviews, coded and analysed using the software NVivo. The video call interviews took place between June and September 2020 with an approximate duration of 90 min according to a script of 12 questions organized in four groups: 1) about the overall concept of the platform; 2) about the content collection; 3) about the filtering, combination and curation processes; 4) about presentation and visualization approaches along with proposals of features and use contexts. The experts were challenged to brainstorm about the concept in the ideation stage, according to their personal and professional experience, as well as encouraged to freely express opinions and suggestions.

Following the qualitative method to content analysis of Laurence Bardin [15], the analysis dimensions defined in the script were subsequently recoded and regrouped after the reading of the full transcripts, that brought unforeseen aspects mentioned by the experts. On the one hand, there was a vertical and subjective analysis of the discourse of each of the interviewees and the richness of their feedback, references and recommendations. On the other hand, a horizontal and transversal overview identifying the most frequent words associated with themes and comparing the emphasis on specific topics and concerns, using NVivo matrix coding queries. This paper presents a segment of the qualitative data gathered through the interviews, focused on the aggregation of tactics to evoke collective memories and encourage participation, that were systematized in recommendations and strategies, presented in the next section.

4.1 Sample Characterization

The sample comprises eleven experts, between 37 and 55 years old, from which five are male and six are female. The criteria for selecting the experts was based on the significance of their theoretical and practical work in relevant projects in Portugal[1], within the areas of archives, museology, heritage, ethnography, community projects, cultural events, design, participatory media and digital platforms. Figure 3 presents the interviewees identified, with an ID and their profiles, grouped according to areas of expertise that let to the identification of two panels: five specialists are oriented towards humanistic and social science domains in the context of cultural and community dynamics – codified as the panel Culture and Communities (CC); five specialists are inscribed in the field of design, digital art and participatory technologies – codified as the panel Platforms and Participation (PP) and; one of the specialists presents a mixed profile (CC/PP). In addition to gathering a set of complementary contributions that are representative of their field, the definition of two panels intended to verify whether there were differences of opinion according to the area of expertise.

---

[1] https://arquivodememoria.pt/; https://campus.altice.pt/; http://center.web.ua.pt/; https://cdv.dei. uc.pt/; https://digitalich.memoriamedia.net/; https://gps.pt/u/ffms; https://www.facebook.com/ GrETUA.oficial/; https://memoriaparatodos.pt/; https://www.memoriamedia.net/; https://2019. portodesignbiennale.pt/; http://wholewebcatalog.org/; https://institutodehistoriadaarte.wordpr ess.com/unplace/.

ID	FIELD OF EXPERTISE
(CC) Culture and Communities Panel	
[CC01]	Graduated in editorial studies, cinema and theater, he is an artistic director and cultural programmer of events in an experimental theater company based in a university community.
[CC02]	Historian and full professor, having been Secretary of State for Science, Technology and Higher Education in Portugal. She is the coordinator of several projects with communities, focused on memory, oral history, life testimonies and citizen science.
[CC03]	Social scientist and researcher focused on sociological and ethnographic work with communities. She is a UNESCO consultant for intangible heritage and was the founder of a multimedia archive linked to Portuguese intangible cultural heritage and founder of an international observatory of digital inventories of Intangible Cultural Heritage.
[CC04]	University professor and researcher on the domain of cultural studies, heritage and museology with particular focus on digital art and cultures, having led research projects on web art and online museography. She was director of a national contemporary art museum and is a member of the research network of the Europeana platform and other networks on digital culture and museums.
[CC05]	Curator, university professor and researcher on design history and theory with particular focus on Portuguese visual and material culture. He is the director of a design research unit and the main curator of a national design biennial.
(CC/PP) Mixed Profile	
[CC/PP06]	Designer in an information technology company specialized in the development of museum and heritage management systems, having developed several projects with communities and memory archives. She is a member of Museums and Web research network and a PhD student with research about augmented reality in museums.
(PP) Platforms and Participation Panel	
[PP07]	Designer, university professor and researcher on visual culture and platform studies using network visualization and machine learning techniques.
[PP08]	Designer, university professor and researcher in the field of branding, participatory design and co-creation, collaborating on several projects on creativity and brand activation.
[PP09]	University professor and researcher in the field of participatory media and digital platforms with several projects linked to online communities and participatory dynamics in education.
[PP10]	University professor and researcher in the field of artificial intelligence and machine learning. He is coordinator of a research unit in the field of computational design and information visualization, in which he coordinates several artistic and R&D projects based on locative technologies, big data computing and artificial intelligence.
[PP11]	Designer, digital artist, university lecturer and researcher in the field of new media. Develops cultural programming and web design projects for associations and cultural entities, and artistic interventions using everyday technology (small technology) and content aggregation tools (mashup tools).

Fig. 3. Experts' profile characterization.

5   Results

5.1   Use Contexts and Audience

Departing from the opinions and suggestions of the experts, one of the categories of analysis was subject to an in-depth interpretation, to refine the core concept and identify relevant use contexts. Within the category dedicated to the "I) Overall Concept of the Platform", the following codes were selected: a) "Use Contexts"; b) "User Profiles"; c)

"Needs and Differentiation" and; d) "Challenges". The combined interpretation of these indicators led to the systematization of specific use contexts mentioned by the experts as useful and innovative. Figure 4 summarizes the identified use contexts associated with particular needs and arranged according to their focus and type of participation (more opened or mediated).

TYPOLOGY	Suggestions of USES CONTEXTS and AUDIENCES

FOCUS: Research and Knowledge

ARCHIVES

Based on existing resources and mostly powered by a niche audience

> **Thematic aggregation platform linked to culture and science** that brings together, organizes, makes available in terms of direct access and discovery related resources dispersed on other platforms, not only visual content but also audio resources thus promoting accessibility (e.g. audio description) | AUDIENCE: researchers and specialized audiences [CC04]

> **Correlated visualizations of documental collections from institutions** (such museums and archives) to generate debate and instigate diverse readings and depictions (e.g. invite curators and other users to create different paths and perspectives on the collections) | AUDIENCE: researchers and audiences interested in a particular topic [CC: 03, 05; PP: 07, 11]

FOCUS: Information and Emotion

PLACES

Coordinated by a local promoter around place-based resources

> **Territory/cultural mapping** promoted by local agents and expanded by inhabitants and users to offer multiple tangible and intangible experiences on the same content, according to a segmentation of audiences | AUDIENCE: local communities and visitors [PP08]

> **Locative and georeferencing tool to collect audiovisual records,** oral testimonies and life stories on the go | AUDIENCE: researchers and communities [CC: 02, 03, 05]

FOCUS: Emotion and Experience

EVENTS

Based on open content sharing including in loco and on the go by different user profiles

> **Platform associated with recurring events,** such as conferences, music festivals and concerts, taking advantage of georeferencing services (e.g. different presentation approaches, stage angles, etc.) and promoting networking among the participants, allowing a quick search for content specific locations, people, previous editions, etc. | AUDIENCE: specialized audiences and fans [PP: 09, 10]

> Platform to document and activate participation associated with recurrent events about **traditions and cultural heritage, allowing to explore their evolution over time and establishing connections between different categories of heritage** (e.g. intangible and, tangible such as movable, immovable, natural, etc.) | AUDIENCE: community and local entities, active participants, researchers, stakeholders, visitors, etc. [CC03; CC/PP06]

> **Mapping and documenting the process of an event,** from the planning to the records of taking place for future memory (e.g. an exhibition, a concert, a show, etc.) | AUDIENCE: authors, artists, curators, staff, hosts, patrons, sponsors, critics, researchers, educational services, audiences, etc. [CC: 01, 05]

Fig. 4. Systematization of use contexts identified by experts

5.2 Strategies to Collect, Visualize and Participate

Towards guiding the next steps with prototypes' evaluation, three categories of analysis were thoroughly examined and translated into operative recommendations: "II) Content Collection Category" with the following codes: "Interoperability and Metadata", "Copyrights and Privacy" and; "Evocative Resources"; the "III) Content Combination Category" with the codes: "Classification and Curation Systems", "Human vs. Automated Curation" and, "Social Activation and Related Content"; the "IV) Content Presentation Category" including the codes: "Visualization Modes", "Content Flow and Update vs. Memory Fixation", "Visual Storytelling, Emotion and Sense of Collective" and, "User Profiles' Literacy and Generational Preferences".

Figure 5 systematizes the formulated strategies expressed by the experts during the interviews. The three core elements – collect, visualize and participate – are intertwined in the concept of the proposed platform, because the upload of content should be possible during the interaction with other content already shared and, therefore influencing the correlated visualizations. In this sense, the three core elements, as well as the recommendations and strategies, are codependent:

- the identification of the relevant **metadata** is associated with **strategies for content collection**, that highlight some features to include in the input form and data retrieving from the media files shared by users;
- the identification of the most effective **resources** to capture experiences and trigger related memories is associated with **strategies for evocation and visual elicitation**, that address approaches in guiding and encouraging meaningful records and also strategies to their presentation aiming to encapsulate the essence of an experience to evoke similar memories and create a sense of collectiveness;
- the identification of the **presentation formats** mentioned by the experts is related with **strategies for visualization models** to structure the archive of resources and provide several ways of navigating and curating, according to filters of interest and layers of information that highlight the similarities but also the diversity of contributions;
- the identification of existing **motivations and opportunities** is associated with **strategies for joining and participating**, that aim to reduce the activation gap that prevents people to adopt and actively contribute and interact with a new system despite their manifest interest, namely through mediation and activation mechanisms.

Metadata

- **people** - author and who is involved (e.g. tagging);
- **source / context** - where it circulated and what discourses generated (e.g. comments);
- **location** - types of places (e.g. airport, beach), granularity (e.g. country, city, neighborhood, coordinates);
- **time** - temporal references (e.g. season, holiday, 'in the 60s'), granularity (e.g. centuries, years, months, days, time of publication);
- **description** - what it is, why it is being shared and what it means for the community and author;
- **categories / keywords** - suggestion of terms defined and/or already inputted by other users (e.g. thesaurus, hastags).

Strategies for content collection

1. Allow **multiple formats** for users to choose how to **better express**;
2. Provide a **guided and concise form** (4 or 5 fields);
3. Aim for metadata **interoperability** (e.g. IIIF Framework; Dublin Core);
4. Provide **flexibility** but assure **info verification**;
5. Extract **data from the media files** (e.g. EXIF);
6. Use **image vision APIs** (e.g. Google Cloud Vision);
7. Adopt **open access** and **clear disclaimers**.

Media Resources

- **First person testimonials** - authenticity and expressiveness;
- **Mediatic content** - massive and repeated circulation in the media;
- **Sound** - gives the surround and evokes context;
- **Short videos** - avert void moments and being too time consuming;
- **Still image** - more open to several interpretations;
- **Text** - personal meanings and emotions.

Strategies for evocation and visual elicitation

1. Evoke **types of experiences** to trigger related memories;
2. Explore memories of **groups** and **mediatic events** that generated multiple opinions;
3. Trigger **affection** to encourage **qualitative translation of information** (e.g. guiding questions and visual elicitation);
4. Encourage **first person testimonials** (authenticity, accent, body expression);
5. Explore **storytelling** to create **empathy, nostalgia** and **appropriation**;
6. Explore a **documental approach** that gives access to the **process** and **multiple sides of a narrative**.

Visual Formats

- **Maps**;
- **Timelines**;
- **Albums** and **Collections**;
- **Media galleries**;
  Feed and wall model
- (e.g. social media profile);
  Image sequences with
- **reactions** (e.g. stories);
  Short animations and
- **videos** (e.g. social media memories).

Strategies for visualization models

1. Consider different **goals** according to **user profiles** (informative, playful, exploratory);
2. Provide **several ways of experiencing content** (e.g. filters and visualizations models);
3. Show **diversity** through **multiple points of view**;
4. Explore **layers** of meaning to enrich the content (e.g. **context, emotion**, etc.);
5. Explore the shifting between **Zoom-out** (overview) and **Zoom-in** (detail);
6. Balance **automatic presentations** with **users' curation**;
7. Explore both **memory activation** (ephemeral mechanisms) and **memory fixation** (the archive).

Opportunities

- Take advantage of the current **predisposition to digital mediation** amplified by the pandemic;
- Target audiences who want to contribute to the **representation of a place or community** (e.g. locals, fans, researchers, etc.);
- Provide **aggregation and organization** of disperse content shared by audiences with common interests;

Strategies for participating

1. Eliminate cost of adoption by being a **plug-in** (e.g. ticketing or adopted **corporate platforms**);
2. Providing **locative features** to use in **face-to-face events**;
3. Highlight the relevance of **people** to the collective and make **UGC** easily **sharable**;
4. Explore **storytelling** and **social media interaction models** (e.g. immediate, expressive, opened to feedback);
5. Promote **call-to-action events** to activate participation and discussion (e.g. thematic triggers, recall cycles, inviting people to curate and moderate);
6. Use **gamification mechanisms** to attract new users and increase interactions (e.g. give access to extras, offer storage space, attribute reputation badges).

Fig. 5. Recommendations and strategies suggested by the experts to apply in the participatory platform.

6 Discussion of Results

Despite the differentiated profile and the separation of the panels, the eclectic and multidisciplinary sample expressed wide-ranging opinions in their discourse, beyond their domain of expertise. Nevertheless, we highlight the main differences identified between the two panels were:

- The panel Culture and Communities (CC) manifested greater enthusiasm towards the concept, although it placed emphasis on the need for human mediation, which should be carried out by the 'event/project promoters' to guarantee the reliability of the information. Also, this panel pointed the importance of having a guiding structure to avoid disperse and decontextualized information that could generate disinformation and would constitute an obstacle to the application of the platform in historical research and in some institutional contexts. In addition, some elements of the CC panel highlighted the need and potential of such a platform to facilitate the collection of testimonies from communities in loco (many at risk of being lost due to the advanced age of their beholders).
- The panel Platforms and Participation (PP) manifested scepticism about people's adherence to another platform, given the required effort and the cost-benefit face to competitors like social media (already with many followers). Also, in institutional uses, open participation may be problematic and require more regulations that may be interpreted as restrictive and less democratic. Hence, instead of pointing to wider audiences, the PP panel suggested more specialized niche uses (particularly targets that already show appreciation for the emotional and techno-aesthetic dimension of the experience as a differentiating feature).

Nevertheless, both panels emphasized the importance of ensuring the transparency of criteria and mechanisms of the platform towards informed participation. Furthermore, all participants were consensual in avoiding algorithmically biased control mechanisms in favour of self-regulation and peer-reviews. Another relevant topic mentioned by some elements, of both panels, was the contemporary interest in accessing invisible dimensions of processes and events (including the making-of and backstage which allow audiences to connect directly with resources and agents in a non-hierarchical way).

Overall, the use contexts and strategies systematized from the experts' contributions aimed at countering overly closed and imposing systems in favour of shared constructions of meaning from multiple perspectives to enhance scientific cooperation as well as co-creation. Besides the distinguishing feature of aiming to generate correlated and meaningful visualizations from UGC, that may contribute to the depiction of collective memories, we can state that the main opportunity for this platform is related to the general need for content aggregation and exploration. However, despite this opportunity and the findings already described, the experts also mentioned some critical challenges that may compromise the platform's sustainability.

Even with the proper resources to implement and maintain this kind of participatory platform is necessary to be aware of the risk of generating conflicts because collective memory is not consensual and, also, to acknowledge the danger of artificial appropriation of events. In this sense, the purposes of use must consider distinguishing between entertaining scenarios (based on immediate gratification and creative derivation) and scenarios of community production of knowledge. Some degree of compatibility of these instances can be possible but will have to be carefully planned, designed and evaluated with users. In any case, an online digital platform does not necessarily become a living archive. To avoid a quick hype followed by lack of interest is vital to assuring mediation and activation strategies (complementary to in-person participation in events). For the next stage is prudent to consider testing prototypes with a niche audience from a cohesive group, concerning topics of their interest. It will be more likely they will be committed to providing reliable information and taking an active part in content activation. After the start-up with mobilized groups to feed the platform and gain scale, it will be more favourable to create relevant partnerships to attract institutional uses.

7 Final Considerations and Future Work

The systematization of the qualitative data gathered from related work and the feedback of experts allowed to achieve the objectives of the paper: consolidate the concept, identify use contexts and provide strategies for prototyping a participatory platform to share and visualize audiovisual collective memories. The adopted methodology privileged a participatory design approach by integrating experts during the ideation stage without restricting their opinions with established decisions about the platform interface and features. The goal was to freely identify needs and cultural contexts of use, based on community dynamics generated by the participants (e.g. events like concerts and exhibitions, intangible heritage and traditional celebrations, oral history, and life stories were suggested by the interviewees). Also, some of the main challenges identified by the experts to develop a solution that brings together researchers and communities are: the reliability and contextualization of resources; the transparency regarding the system mechanisms and operations; the sustainability to feed and maintain the system alive without becoming a storage repository; the balance between spontaneous and specialized discourses and; the balance between the design of a simple interface and the features required to make it a useful tool, without neutralizing the emotional drive of capturing meaningful experiences to become collective and cherished memories. Worthy of particular mention is this emotional dimension of the experience and the fact that the sense of collective memory will hardly be consensual, static or well defined. Hence, this will also be a relevant qualitative topic to be explored in focus groups of potential users, to complement and corroborate the experts' insights.

In sum, the operative contributes to guide the prototype development to be tested with users are a set of use contexts (**Archives-driven, focused on Research and Knowledge** – based on existing resources and mostly powered by a niche audience; **Places-driven, focused on Information and Emotion** – coordinated by local promoters; **Events-driven, focused on Emotion and Experience** – Based on open and in loco content sharing by different user profiles) together with recommendations and strategies to guide the development process (relevant **metadata** associated with **strategies for content collection**; effective **resources** to capture experiences associated with **strategies for evocation and visual elicitation**; **presentation formats** related with **strategies for visualization models** and; **motivations and opportunities** associated with **strategies for joining and participating**). Furthermore, we hope these findings may also be helpful for other participatory projects focused on collective experiences combining several resources, that can be preserved, represented and shared as meaningful and insightful memories within communities.

Acknowledgments. The research is funded by FCT - Fundação para a Ciência e a Tecnologia (Grant nr. SFRH/BD/132780/2017). The authors acknowledge the collaboration of the experts.

References

1. Olsson, T.: Understanding collective content: purposes, characteristics and collaborative practices. In: Proceedings of the Fourth International Conference on Communities and Technologies, C&T 2009, pp. 21–30. University Park, PA, USA (2009). https://doi.org/10.1145/155 6460.1556464
2. Jenkins, H.: Convergence Culture: Where Old and New Media Collide. New York University Press, New York (2008)
3. Segel, E., Heer, J.: Narrative visualization: telling stories with data. IEEE Trans. Vis. Comput. Graph. **16**(6), 1139–1148 (2010). https://doi.org/10.1109/TVCG.2010.179
4. Ovaskainen, E.: 9 Types of Visual Storytelling on Mobile. In Global Investigative Journalism Network. 2 January 2019. https://gijn.org/2019/01/02/9-types-of-visual-storytelling-on-mob ile/. Accessed 13 Nov 2020
5. Nordström, M.: A case study in social media mashup concept validation. Master thesis. Aalto University - School of Science and Technology, Helsinki (2010)
6. Lévy, P.: Collective Intelligence: Mankind's Emerging World in Cyberspace. Helix Books (1999)
7. Alexander, B.: The New Digital Storytelling - Creating Narratives with New Media. Praeger, Santa Barbara, California (2011)
8. Tufte, E.: The Visual Display of Quantitative Information. Graphics Press, Cheshire (1983)
9. Tufte, E.R.: Envisioning Information. Graphics Press, Cheshire (1990)
10. Shneiderman, B.: The eyes have it: a task by data type taxonomy for information visualizations. In: IEEE Symposium on Visual Languages Proceedings, pp. 336–343 (1996). https://doi.org/10.1109/VL.1996.545307
11. Meirelles, I.: Design for Information. An Introduction to the Histories, Theories, and Best Practices Behind Effective Information Visualizations. Rockport Publishers, Gloucester, Massachusetts (2013)
12. Pousman, Z., Stasko, J., Mateas, M.: Casual information visualization: depictions of data in everyday life. IEEE Trans. Vis. Comput. Graph. **13**(6), 1145–1152 (2007). https://doi.org/10.1109/TVCG.2007.70541
13. Glaser, B.G., Strauss, A.L.: The Discovery of Grounded Theory - Strategies for Qualitative Research. Routledge, London (2017)
14. Simonsen, J., Robertson, T.: Routledge International Handbook of Participatory Design. Routledge, London (2013)
15. Bardin, L.: Análise de Conteúdo. Edições 70, Almedina Brasil, São Paulo (2011)

Content Aggregation on Streaming Media Devices: Assessment of Four Popular Market Solutions

Bernardo Cardoso$^{(\boxtimes)}$ ⓘ and Jorge Abreu ⓘ

Digimedia, Department of Communication and Arts, University of Aveiro,
3810-193 Aveiro, Portugal
{bernardoc,jfa}@ua.pt

Abstract. The variety of video content sources is increasing every day, ranging from linear broadcast TV to multiple providers of video streaming over the
internet, either over-the-top (OTT) platforms or user-generated content (UGC).
However, most of this content is made available to the users in completely discon-
nected ways, even when provided on the same device, mostly due to the app-based
nature of current offerings. A short time ago the research team of the UltraTV
project found that users were keen to try more unified ways to access audiovisual content. This paper revisits content unification, a major topic on the UltraTV
research agenda, by assessing how major contemporary commercial video platforms, in this case, the four most popular streaming media devices (SMD) in
North America, addresses the most noteworthy topics of UltraTV content integration concepts: multi-source content discovery, integration vs multi-app approach,
transversal search, embedded player vs deep linking, and multi-profile support.

Keywords: Content integration · Content unification · Content aggregation ·
Streaming media devices · UltraTV

1 Introduction

In 2016, a consortium of academic research labs and a major IPTV provider in Portugal
embarked on a multi-year project to create a new Interactive TV (iTV) platform. This
project, christened UltraTV [1], was quite ambitious, targeting several research topics,
including a disruptive new User Interface (UI). However, one of the most interesting
aspects was the focus in fusing linear and non-linear content, from a multichannel video
programming distributor (MVPD) with over-the-top (OTT) sources, like Netflix, but
also user-generated content (UGC) from platforms like YouTube and even audiovisual
content from social networks, like Facebook Video, all in a seamless interface. UltraTV
content unification research sought to understand if the users were pleased with the
multi-app approach, that started to carry over from the mobile world into the connected
TV world [2] or if they were receptive to a much more integrated way to consume their
preferred video content. At the time, and despite the constraints of this research project,
it was found that a majority of users would prefer an integrated approach [3].

© Springer Nature Switzerland AG 2021
M. J. Abásolo et al. (Eds.): jAUTI 2020, CCIS 1433, pp. 15–27, 2021.
https://doi.org/10.1007/978-3-030-81996-5_2

This paper aims to revisit the concept of content unification, raised by the UltraTV project, and compare the most important features of that project with a set of relevant offerings in the current market, to understand how the industry aligned with those concepts that have the potential to keep the TV set as the preferred device to watch audiovisual content at home [4, 5]. For this assessment, the four most popular streaming media devices (SMD), excluding SmartTVs, in North America were selected, namely: Roku, Apple TV, Amazon Fire TV, and Chromecast/Google TV [6].

With a focus on understanding how UltraTV and these four SMDs cater to the concept of content integration while addressing the three main content watching activities, discovering, viewing and following content, five topics were selected for a hands-on analysis:

- The general UI concept for content browse and discovery on the platform;
- The extent of content integration, either built directly into the platform or by using an app-based approach;
- The support for transversal search with multiple content sources;
- The way the content viewing is handled, either through deep linking to the assets or by reproducing content in an integrated player at the platform level;
- The approach for multiple user-profiles and how profile switching is handled at the platform level and inside the apps.

The first three topics of analysis are associated with the "discovering content" activity. In the initial topic, the main UI model for browsing content inside the platform will be evaluated, since browsing is usually the way most users select something to watch. Next, in the case that content is not surfaced in the main UI because the SMD is app-based and thus mostly siloed, the aim will be to understand how content from different sources could be presented to the user. That is, identify if the platform has some kind of aggregator app [2], for the user to browse different catalogs in an integrated way. Lastly, and being "search" the main alternative to "browse", understand where the platform does support a search functionality and whether it can simultaneously search for content in multiple catalogs.

On the "content viewing" activity the main focus will be to understand if there is an integrated player at the platform level, at the aggregator app level or if the watching always happened inside separated players on the 3rd party apps. In the latter case, the analysis will also address the ability of the platform to deep link directly to content.

For the "following content" activity the aim was to spot the SMDs approach to such concepts as "following a series", "continue watching", "watch lists", "favorite lists" or recommendations, usually perceived as the personalization features of a platform. Most importantly, the analysis will address how those functionalities are integrated into the platform and if there is support for distinct user-profiles. Additionally, the multiple profiles feature will be analyzed to access if it extends from the platform level and reaches the apps that also have this functionality. That is, evaluate if when the profile is changed at the platform level this alteration extends to the integrated 3rd party apps or sources like YouTube and Netflix.

This paper starts by presenting, in Sect. 2, how the UltraTV project addressed each of these topics, to better contextualize what was the idea behind each feature. It then proceeds to present the evaluation of each SMD platform and a comparison table in Sect. 3. The paper finish with a brief conclusion on the way the current trend aligned with the approach proposed on the UltraTV project or, on the contrary if the evolution, shaped by the correspondent business models, followed a completely different path.

2   Content Integration on the UltraTV Project

The UltraTV project fully embraced content unification. With that in mind, it was designed from the beginning to fusion linear and on-demand content, from traditional TV and internet-based OTT providers, but also user-generated content (UGC) from platforms like YouTube and social network videos from Facebook Video. In that way, its approach to browse and discovery puts all content at the same level, in a UI that positions a personalized linear TV selection front-center, surrounded to the right with two personalized playlists, one for on-demand traditional TV content and other for internet content sources. The UI allowed also a more traditional organization style, by having broadcast content categorized by genre in the columns to the left of these central personalized lists. OTT content is found in the columns on the right side arranged by provider[1] (see Fig. 1).

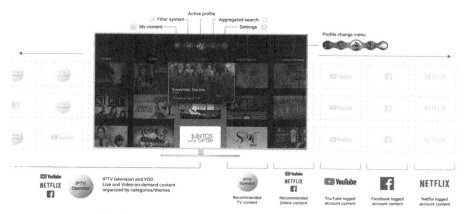

Fig. 1. UltraTV main approach to browse and discovery

When the UltraTV project was conceived, it anticipated an app-based approach as the way to integrate additional features into the system. The idea was to make it simpler to integrate non-content related capabilities, like e-health and e-learning features. However, since the inception, the vision of adding more content or content sources to the platform was to be a fully integrated one, that would not need the addition of specialized apps.

However, to be able to incorporate, in a meaningful way, distinct content sources, the project needed to ingest and process all their metadata: titles, synopses, directors, actors, airing dates, seasons, episodes and so on. The project had access to the basic linear and on-demand content metadata provided by the MVPD. Yet, this metadata is traditionally

---

[1] https://www.youtube.com/watch?v=xg6MHYxhxyQ.

segregated between what is usually called EPG listings for linear, and VOD or catalog metadata for on-demand content. These two data sources were reconciled by linking the linear programs with their catch-up counterparts and normal VOD assets. Netflix catalog was integrated in a similar way, creating a unified database. Understandably, this approach was not followed in the integration of YouTube and Facebook assets, given the sheer dimension of such catalogs. For these two services the approach was to integrate only a small subset of their top categories, that is, the categories that are usually highlighted in a non-personalized way on the main UI of these UGC platforms.

This unified metadata database was used to implement the cross-origin content columns on UltraTV browse UI. However, the multi-source search functionality, besides using the database, also performed online video searches in YouTube and Facebook Video and merged the different results on-the-fly, to allow the presentation of a unified search experience.

UltraTV content consumption was designed around the concept of an integrated player experience, and in that way detached itself from the usual app-based platforms, that make the user bounce from app to app in order to be able to watch different content. In the project context, this approach was successful except for playing Netflix assets. In that case, a deep linking solution was employed. Having almost all content reproduced directly inside the UltraTV main interface created an immersive experience, that blended the different content sources in the same UI. The integrated player nature of UltraTV also allowed the system to present cross-origin recommendations directly in the player UI, and to collect analytics on the consumption of 3rd party OTT content.

UltraTV approach to multi-profiles was quite advanced for the time, having concepts like group profiles to better address the communal aspect of watching TV on a big screen. An innovative feature was the notion of account linking, where it allowed a user to connect his UltraTV profile to their Netflix, YouTube and Facebook accounts. That way when a user changes his/her profile, the system automatically refreshes itself and fetches personalized content, not only from the UltraTV recommender but also from the different OTT and UGC providers [7].

3   Assessment of Four Popular SMDs in North America

3.1   Roku

The Roku platform started as a project to bring Netflix to the big screen (at a time when it was just available on web browsers) and evolved to represent the most popular SMD platform in North America [6], with its multiple models of inexpensive STBs (Set-top Boxes), streaming sticks and software for connected TVs. In Roku, the general UI concept is one of simplicity, with the main menu on the left and a grid of icons to the right of it, see Fig. 2a). Since the beginning Roku tried to make things simpler for the big screen TV user, that is why their apps are called "Channels", to keep an easy mental link to a traditional TV set. Roku partners and producers create these "Channels" and publish them through a store, called "Channel Store". However, since these "Channels" behave just like apps in other platforms, in the sense that they carry not only distinct content, but also have dissimilar UIs and UXs, the whole Roku platform can be considered app-based.

Even with an app-based approach, Roku still has some content aggregation functionalities. One of these is the "Roku Channel", an app created by Roku itself, that aggregates content curated and licensed by Roku from different partners, both linear and on-demand, see Fig. 2b). This makes Roku not only a platform owner but also an OTT operator itself. For instance, the "Roku Channel" also exists as an app for Android, iOS and even Amazon Fire TV. While inside this app, the content is reproduced in an integrated player and there is no deep linking, even for content from partners that also have standalone apps in the platform, like HBO or Showtime. In that respect, the "Roku Channel" is not really aggregating content surfaced by the different sources that are available in the Roku platform. In reality, it is just like any other content app and has a business model based on advertising for the content that it makes available for free. However, the "Roku Channel" also allows the user to subscribe inside de app to additional premium content, from providers like Showtime, AMC or Starz, creating an additional revenue stream to Roku. This addition of premium subscription content, curated and billed by Roku on the "Roku Channel" to the free ad-supported content, makes this platform looks more and more like an OTT MVPD [2], Fig. 2c). The major streaming platform absent from such integration is Netflix.

a) Main Menu

b) The Roku Channel

c) Premium Subscriptions

d) Search

Fig. 2. Roku UI

One of the more unifying features on the Roku platform is, however, its cross-app search. Roku works with the app creators, so they provide Roku with metadata feeds for the content available inside their respective apps, Fig. 2d). If the same content is present in more than one source, the search interface presents distinct alternatives for the user to choose. However, the playing itself, when initiated thru the search function, is then handled in each of the separated apps via deep linking and not played in an immersive way like in the "Roku Channel".

An innovative personalization feature leveraged by these metadata feeds is a "follow" functionality integrated on the platform. For instance, when using the transversal search, a user can follow a movie, a series or even a person, and be notified on the "My Feed" menu item about changes on these topics, like new episodes available or price changes.

What Roku lacks is any feature related to profiles. A Roku account is needed for the initial setup, but changing the account requires a factory reset of the device. The apps that allow multiple profiles still support them, but on an app-by-app basis, like Netflix or YouTube, not as a platform profile. Also, there are limited personalized content recommendations on the platform, instead promoted and highlighted content seems to be mostly curated.

3.2 Apple TV

Apple TV evolved from being a "hobby" for Apple [8], to be the 2nd most popular SMD platform in North America [6]. With the launch of the 4th generation in 2015, this small STB got a UI redesign paired with a brand new remote, that still today is not consensual. The main STB UI has a big area on top, called "top shelf", providing a way for the apps that have a privileged spot on the first row to promote their contents or functionalities. Below there are rows of app icons, or app groups, much like in an iPhone or iPad. Besides the "top shelf" that itself is app-driven, there is no content surfaced on the main Apple TV interface, so this platform is clearly app-based, see Fig. 3a).

Content aggregation really happens inside what Apple calls the "TV" app. On this app, which mimics the main Apple TV UI, the user can browse for content provided by Apple itself, from its "Apple TV+" OTT platform or made available by partner apps or other content sources, see Fig. 3b). This content populates the main "TV" app UI and special thematic sections with areas dedicated, for example, to sports (including live broadcasts) or kids.

Similar to Roku, Apple gets metadata about the content provided by other apps thru a server-to-server feed integration [9]. However, instead of using this metadata feed only for a cross-app search, Apple uses it to make the "TV" app a showcase of the content the user can access on the platform, behaving in this respect as a content discovery application [2]. Most of this content, when activated is then reproduced inside the respective apps via deep linking directly to the content. A nice feature, resulting from the server-to-server feed integration is that the user does not need to have all the apps installed for the content to be showcased and highlighted on the "TV" app. However, when a user tries to play content that does not have the correspondent app installed, he/she is redirected to the App Store for the download and installation.

But, more than that, Apple establishes partnerships with 3rd party content producers and OTT platforms to extend this discovery behavior into a full fledge content aggregation platform. Inside the "TV" app, in a feature called "Channels", there are subscriptions to additional content, which the viewer can use to expand their "TV" app catalog, see Fig. 3c). This makes Apple and the "TV" app also some sort of new OTT MVPD, not much different than a traditional cable operator, and similar to the "Roku Channel" [10]. But, besides the business aspect, "… unlike discovery apps, aggregator apps enable users

a) Home Screen   b) "TV" app

c) "TV" app "Channels"   d) Search

Fig. 3. Apple TV UI

to watch content from other providers within the interface of their app" [2: 175]. This is a crucial improvement from the UX perspective and implies a big departure from the app hopping approach typical of this platform. However, as in Roku case, Netflix is notoriously absent from that deep integration.

Apple TV has two separated search functions, at the platform level, there is a "Search" app that, as the name suggests, does a cross-app search, but is not restricted to audiovisual content, searching also in iTunes catalog for music albums and songs, or in the App Store for apps and games. But inside the "TV" app there is also a search function, that in this case is focused on searching for movies, shows, cast and crew from multiple content sources, Fig. 3d).

In terms of personalization functions, with all the information that Apple collects from the content consumed inside the "TV" app, and from the deep linking partners that share back to Apple information about assets watched inside their apps, the "TV" app can present a fully integrated "Continue Watch" list.

Recent versions of the Apple TV platform do have the notion of multiple user-profiles, however, the current materialization is mostly limited to the Apple ecosystem. For instance, when the user changes profiles, the set of installed apps changes automatically on the main UI. Similarly, the signed-in user on Apple services (iTunes, Apple TV+, etc.) also changes. Inside the "TV" app, the "Continue Watch" rail and the curated sections also reflect the usage made by the different profiles. However, there is no linking between the Apple TV profile and the profiles inside other apps, e.g., changing from profile A to profile B on the Apple TV UI will have no impact on the selected profile or account on the Disney+ app or the YouTube app.

3.3 Amazon Fire TV

Amazon Fire TV is a diversified line of SMDs made by Amazon. They are little powerful devices a bit more expensive than Roku. The general UI concept for the main screen in Fire TV is split into 3 areas, see Fig. 4a). It has a top main menu, followed by a big area that when selected, automatically starts playing a trailer, a promotional video, or a static banner. Below that promotional area, there are rows of items, that have different functions depending on the usage given to the SMD.

a) Home Screen

b) IMDb TV app

c) Prime Video app "Channels"

d) Search

Fig. 4. Amazon Fire TV UI

Since the underlying software of Fire TV is based on Android, its main approach is app-based. The system gets a lot of Amazon apps pre-installed, side by side to the usual Netflix and YouTube apps. Throughout the platform, it is easy to see that Amazon content and products have a very prominent position, and this is leveraged, mostly by pushing Amazon Prime Video content up and center. Nevertheless, the rows of tiles in the main screen and in the different tabs from the top menu surface a mix of promoted content and apps from Amazon and its partners. This means that even with an app-based platform there is a lot of content scattered all over the UI, implying that there is a strong connection between Fire TV and content discovery and consumption.

But Amazon approach to content discovery goes beyond the main Fire TV UI, it actually has two additional aggregation apps. Similar to the "Roku Channel", where the user can watch free ad-based content, Amazon provides an IMDb TV app, see Fig. 4b) [11], and like with the "Roku Channel" this app is also available outside the Fire TV ecosystem. Content available in the IMDb TV app is reproduced in an integrated player, transversal to the platform, and movies and series not watched to the end are surfaced to a special "Recent" rail, on the main Fire TV UI, that works as a cross-app "Continue Watch" functionality. The same happens with Prime Video content watched on the Prime Video app. However, this does not extend to other apps like Netflix or YouTube, in that case just the app icon appears on the "Recent" rail, not the content itself. The same applies to the actual content playing, where apps outside of the Amazon ecosystem reproduce content thru deep linking and not in the same integrated player that the apps from Amazon use.

The major app Amazon has on the platform is the Prime Video app. It is similar to the "TV" app in the Apple TV, working also as an aggregator app, providing under a subscription not only content produced and licensed by Amazon as an OTT platform but also allowing users to top up this subscription with additional partner contents, from producers like HBO, Showtime, etc. Just like Apple, Amazon calls these additional content sources "Channels", see Fig. 4c), and this also transforms Amazon, much like Roku and Apple, into a kind of OTT MVPD. Again, like in the other two cases, Netflix is absent from this bundling.

Amazon Fire TV, like the other SMDs, uses metadata feeds to surface content from the different apps and partners. That metadata is used by the main UI but also on the search function, see Fig. 4d). Since Amazon has many partners, and is business-driven, when content is selected either from the search function or from the multiple discovery options a wide range of watching options are presented to the user, either to subscribe, rent or buy. Again, similar to Roku and Apple, these metadata feeds allow Fire TV to index movies and series from apps not yet installed and to promote their installation on-the-fly.

Where the search function stands out is on the relations established between the different content. Using very detailed data from IMDb, the system cross-references actors and directors to create links between the different movies and series. This deep metadata integration extends to the player itself, in a functionality called X-Ray. In some content this allows the user to get information about the actors and characters in a scene, along with other snippets of information like the music track used.

On the personalization features, the main functionality is the, already alluded, cross-app "Recent" rail on the main interface Home screen. The IMDb app has a "Continue Watching" feature and the Prime Video app a similar one called "Watch next", and both share some of the items. However, since the platform has no notion of multiple profiles and even the Prime Video app only got user-profiles recently [12], there is no account linking, with each application managing its own profiles.

3.4 Chromecast and Google TV

Google has the 4th most popular SMD platform in North America [6]. However, this could be a little misleading because most of these devices are Chromecast devices, little dongles, sold directly by Google, and allowing only content reproduction, without a discovery interface and no remote control, making comparisons difficult. Content browse and discovery must be conducted on a PC or mobile device and then sent to be played on the Chromecast device (by "casting" it). Parallelly, Google also develops an Android-based TV software platform, aptly named Android TV, that is used by some hardware partners to create SMDs (NVidia Shield or Xiaomi Mi Box) and SmartTVs (Sony or

Hisense). This hardware and software blend creates a full-featured platform, mostly app-based, that is purchasable directly by end-users but also used by IPTV operators as a basis for their offerings.

Recently, Google launched a new product called Chromecast with Google TV [13], which is really Android TV, with a new interface, running also in a small dongle, but this time with a remote control. This is Google attempt to compete in the same market as the other three platforms with a similar offering, and with a strong emphasis on content.

The main UI concept on Google TV is similar to Amazon Fire TV, with a top main menu, a big slideshow area for promotional content and rows of items, see Fig. 5a).

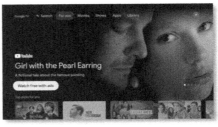

a) "For You" Screen   b) Free premium content on YouTube

c) Cross-app "Continue Watching"   d) Search

Fig. 5. Google TV UI

In this case, Google TV has a first row with personalized recommendations, followed by a row of user apps and then several rows of content arranged by categories or themes making content a first-class citizen, relegating apps to a secondary position. This makes Google TV UI the main way to discover content, and Google promotes it as a hub for accessing all the different streaming platforms in one place. The search function is also well developed and, similarly to the other SMDs, enables cross-app search and can propose alternative ways to purchase or rent the content when available in more than one partner. A feature not easily seen in other SMDs is the ability to search for concepts like "drama movies" or "comedy shows". Being the owner of YouTube means that, most of the times, when a search does not get to a single piece of content, either because it did not find anything on the catalog, or inversely it finds many items, there is always a set of YouTube items provided alongside the main ones, see Fig. 5d).

The playing of content is almost all done via deep linking, even when the content belongs to the Google ecosystem, like YouTube. A little bit strange at first is that in this platform Google enables some premium content, like Hollywood movies, to be played legally for free, with ads, in YouTube, see Fig. 5b).

Google also proposes personalization as a main feature, by having an automatically generated "For you" tab in the default landing page, that focus the catalog on content for which the user does have installed apps. Additionally, in the "Library" tab there is a "Watchlist" function. The user can populate this list with items he finds browsing the unified catalog. The platform also supports a cross-app "Continue watching" list, with partner apps reporting back to Google the consumptions done inside their apps, see Fig. 5c). There is no profile support yet on Google TV [14]. The personalization only applies to a single master account and there is no linking between this account and the profiles used inside the YouTube or Netflix apps.

3.5 Comparison Table

To help with the comparison between the 5 evaluated platforms and the 5 selected research topics, Table 1 summarizes their different approaches.

Table 1. Comparison between UltraTV and the four SMDs

Research topics/Platforms	Browse and discovery	Apps	Cross-search	Content viewing	User profiles
UltraTV	Content-rich UI	App supported	Yes	Predominantly immersive	Multiple profiles & account linking
Roku	The Roku Channel	App-based	Yes	Predominantly deep linking	No profiles
Apple TV	"TV" App	App-based	Yes	Predominantly deep linking	Multiple profiles only on Apple ecosystem
Fire TV	Content-rich UI	App-based	Yes	Predominantly deep linking	No profiles
Google TV	Content-rich UI	App-based	Yes	Predominantly deep linking	Single profile

In this systematization it can be seen that the platforms have a strong alignment in the way that they address content unification, being UltraTV the most contrasting one. The concept of user-profiles is the one where there is the main variation between all the platforms and where the biggest future improvements are expected [12, 14].

4   Conclusion

Content unification and aggregation features are gaining strong traction on the four evaluated platforms. For instance, transversal search functions are currently universally available using metadata feeds from different partners. Still, they lack a deeper integration with non-curated content like YouTube (except for Google TV) or with other social networks, that UltraTV promoted.

These four platforms are mostly app-based, and the additional integration and unification are being promoted thru the creation of special apps like "Roku Channel", Prime Video app and Apple "TV" app. With this strategy, the big players are making those apps silos of deeper integration and personalization, more than endorsing these features to the platform as a whole. For instance, these apps promote an integrated play experience where the platform itself mostly push for deep linking solutions.

On additional personalization features, Fire TV has a "Recent" rail which presents previously watched content and apps. Apple "TV" app goes even further by presenting a transversal "Continue Watching" feature with data shared backed by multiple partners. Google TV, besides also having a "Continue Watching" feature, has a personalized "For You" area that brings recommendations and personalization to the main UI.

Nonetheless, UltraTV although conceived more than three years ago, still had a set of personalization features not broadly available in the market. One of the most notorious was the profile linking, which allowed the platform to automatically expose on the main UI the profiles built into the different partner apps. This made personalization not only a feature of the different apps but also a functionality of the platform itself and made profile changing much easier for the user. Yet, taking into account the progress being made in the contemporary SMDs this will be a deeply welcomed function to foster the TV set as the primary device to watch audiovisual content at home.

An additional research topic, already raised in [2], is that these four SMDs and their respective support platforms are positioning themselves to play the role of MVPDs of the OTT world. They are stockpiling content rights from multiple sources while commissioning exclusive content. They are also working as the bundling partner for additional premium content providers like Showtime and Starz. With that, they are not working just as paywalls, they are creating an immersive UX around a large enough set of content. This could in the future keep the user always inside their walled garden experience, with all its potential harms and benefits.

References

1. UltraTV: UltraTV - Ecossistema de TV de nova geração. http://www.alticelabs.com/site/ult ratv/. Accessed 27 Feb 2021
2. Johnson, C.: The appisation of television: TV apps, discoverability and the software, device and platform ecologies of the internet era. Crit. Stud. Telev. **15**, 165–182 (2020). https://doi.org/10.1177/1749602020911823
3. Velhinho, A., Fernandes, S., Abreu, J., Almeida, P., Silva, T.: Field trial of a new iTV approach: the potential of its UX among younger audiences. In: Abásolo, M.J., Silva, T., González, N.D. (eds.) jAUTI 2018. CCIS, vol. 1004, pp. 131–147. Springer, Cham (2019). https://doi.org/10.1007/978-3-030-23862-9_10
4. Ofcom: Media Nations 2020: UK report. 1 (2020)
5. Comscore: Comscore Reports Surging Levels of In-Home Data Usage. https://www.comscore.com/Insights/Press-Releases/2020/3/Comscore-Reports-Surging-Levels-of-In-Home-Data-Usage. Accessed 23 Nov 2020
6. TiVo: Video Trends Report Q1 (2020)

7. Almeida, P., de Abreu, J., Fernandes, S., Oliveira, E.: Content unification in ITV to enhance user experience: the UltraTV project. In: Proceedings of the 2018 ACM International Conference on Interactive Experiences for TV and Online Video, pp. 167–172. Association for Computing Machinery, New York (2018). https://doi.org/10.1145/3210825.3213558

8. Bilton, N.: "Apple TV is Just a Hobby": How an Argument with Steve Jobs Explains the Future of Apple (2019)

9. Apple: Apple TV App and Universal Search Video Integration - Part 1. https://developer.apple.com/videos/play/tech-talks/508/. Accessed 23 Nov 2020

10. Niu, E.: Apple's vision for the future of television is stuck in the past. https://www.fool.com/investing/2019/03/26/apples-vision-for-the-future-of-television-is-stuc.aspx. Accessed 01 Feb 2021

11. Humphries, M.: Amazon Rebrands IMDb Freedive as IMDb TV, Triples Content (2019)

12. Alexander, J.: Amazon Prime Video is introducing individual user profiles. https://www.theverge.com/2020/7/7/21315370/amazon-prime-video-user-profiles-kids-household-wallet-sharing. Accessed 23 Nov 2020

13. Welch, C.: Google Chromecast (2020) Review: Reinvented — and Now with a Remote. https://www.theverge.com/21495609/google-chromecast-2020-review-streaming-remote-control. Accessed 23 Nov 2020

14. Google: Add accounts on your Google TV. https://support.google.com/googletv/answer/10050564. Accessed 23 Nov 2020

Design and Development of iTV Applications

Design and Implementation of a EWBS Gateway over an IP Telephone Network

Gonzalo Olmedo$^{(\boxtimes)}$, Yeslie Sambrano, Freddy Acosta, and Nancy Paredes

WiCOM-Energy Research Group, Department of Electrical,
Electronics and Telecommunications, Universidad de las Fuerzas Armadas ESPE,
Sanqolquí, Ecuador
{gfolmedo,ynsambrano,fracosta,niparedes}@espe.edu.ec

Abstract. Being part of the so-called "Pacific Ring of Fire" and "Belt of Low Pressure," Ecuador is located in one area most likely to suffer seismic, volcanic, and hydrometeorological threats, which make it possible to catalog as a country with a high vulnerability. For this reason, the use of alert systems such as Emergency Warning Broadcasting System EWBS is necessary for the face of one of these threats, which can be implemented in analog and digital broadcast signals such as Digital Terrestrial Television. In an emergency, the receivers compatible with the EWBS are currently the decoders or digital televisions that include this system. They turn on automatically and emit a visual and audible alert signal that gives time to the population to act more quickly to an event. This article presents the design proposal of a receiver that replicates the warning emergency alert EWBS for digital terrestrial television with the ISDB-Tb standard, through an institutional telephone PBX, implementing an IP telephony server that receives the EWBS system and replicates it to landlines, infocast systems, and mobile phones connected to it, thus avoiding a percentage of losses in the economic and human fields.

Keywords: EWBS · Spatial data infrastructure · Common alert protocol · Risk management

1 Introduction

Earthquakes, volcanic eruptions, floods, forest fires, and landslides are just a few examples of natural disasters for which humans must be prepared. Years ago, people could not predict the dangers mentioned above, so they felt vulnerable and unprotected. However, we have always been aware of the importance of alerting people as quickly as possible to an emerging event to reduce losses and increase opportunities for survival. Over time, with the growth of civilization and the evolution of technology and science, human beings as such have been developing various methods of warning for their protection, such as early warning systems, which are now in continuous change.

As a background to early warning systems or EWS, we had in 1998 the International Conference on EWS EWC 98 defined these systems as a prevention

© Springer Nature Switzerland AG 2021
M. J. Abásolo et al. (Eds.): jAUTI 2020, CCIS 1433, pp. 31–44, 2021.
https://doi.org/10.1007/978-3-030-81996-5_3

element within national and international strategies. In 2003, the Second International Conference on EWS EWCII 03 included that early warning systems should be integrated into countries' public policies. In 2005, the Hyogo Framework for Action 2005–2015 proposed identifying the risks to which each nation is vulnerable and strengthening early warning systems to reduce the percentage of disasters that natural phenomena can cause. It was also stressed that the development of early warning systems should be people-centered. In 2015, the Sendai Framework for Disaster Risk Reduction 2015–2030 proposed significantly increasing access to and availability of early warning systems for multiple natural disasters.

One of the most recognized early warning systems worldwide is that implemented on television and radio receivers with the Integrated Emergency Broadcast Warning System (EWBS), launched in Japan in September 1985 and first used in 1987 emergency experienced by the Japanese people due to a tsunami. In 2000, EWBS was implemented in the Digital Satellite Television (ISDB-S), and in 2003 in the Digital Terrestrial Television (ISDB-T) standard. Since then, the system has warned of natural disasters more than 15 times, giving the population some time to take protective measures [1].

Ecuador has experienced several natural disasters in recent years, the most serious to date being the earthquake that occurred on 16 April 2016 in Pedernales Manabí, which reached a magnitude of 7.8. Nine days after the event, 655 people died, 48 disappeared, and 1,663 were injured [2]. The active stratovolcano "Cotopaxi" has been monitored since 1976 because it is one of the most dangerous volcanoes in the world due to the frequency of its eruptions, with the last one occurring in 2015, and because of the number of populations exposed to its threats [3], including the community of the University of the Armed Forces - ESPE.

Due to events like the previous ones, the EWBS is being integrated into new devices that alert the population, as it is the case of Peru that in October 2015 with the JICA (Japan International Cooperation Agency) and the INICTEL-UNI (National Institute of Investigation and Training of Telecommunications - National University of Engineering), a module and an EWBS chip were used for the development of receivers incorporated in horns, which were used in a simulation of an earthquake of magnitude of 8.5° followed by a tsunami, which counted with the participation of approximately 10 million people. The purpose of this system is that the horns will be used as community alarms for future events that Peru may witness [4].

Since 2016, in Ecuador, the emergency alert system EWBS broadcast tests for digital terrestrial television have been carried out with the ISDB-Tb standard. In [5] the field tests of the Emergency Warning Broadcast System (EWBS) in Quito were presented, integrated into the international ISDB-T digital terrestrial television system. These field tests were made through the broadcasting signal of a commercial channel on 635,143 MHz frequency, in UHF band channel 41. An EWBS server was implemented in the transmitter, where the physical locations that will be alerted were configured, through 12-bit codes defined by cantons for Ecuador in the Harmonization Document Part 3 "EWBS" [6], as well as also the edition of the alert message that will be displayed on the television superimposed on the video and audio signal of the programming, under the ARIB STD-B14 standard [7]. The server reconfigures the PSI/SI tables. It generates a Transport Stream (TS) that is multiplexed with the content of the television channel is transmitted as Broadcast Transport Stream (BTS) together with the emergency bit of the physical layer through a microwave link to the modulator located on Pichincha hill and by broadcast transmission distributed throughout the city. The EWBS server configuration was performed using a remote desktop to the EWBS server located in the television station, activating the emergency alert signal in the receivers located in the city with a delay of less than one second.

The successful experience of testing the EWBS system generated the requirement for a single platform led by the National Service for Risk of Ecuador and Emergency Management that configures the codes of the country's cantons and the editing of the emergency message on the servers that will be installed on television channels, in an agile and dynamic way. In [8] the first results obtained from the integration of the emergency alert system platform that centralizes for EWBS servers were presented. In this platform, a Common Alert Protocol (CAP) [9, 10] module in a Spatial Data Infrastructure (SDI) for risk management and integration of the EWBS System for digital terrestrial television were implemented. As a result of this work, a WEB service shown in Fig. 1 was obtained that contains the EWBS codes representing the cantons of Ecuador, selected through the use of a map viewer of the SDI UCuenca code generator system. The WEB service is consumed by the EWBS server developed by the ESPE University presented in [5], which is in charge of processing the information necessary to transmit an alert via DTT to the cantons that have been selected in the map viewer from SDI UCuenca [11]. The results of the latest EWBS tests carried out in Ecuador at the end of 2019 are presented in the following link: https://youtu.be/ZzBLg3oJbXU.

Increasing the availability of the EWBS systems depends not only on the generation of new transmission systems but also on all the utilities that can be derived from them. It is necessary to identify the transmission and reception protocols, where it is essential to define the transmission mode and the type of receivers. In the first case, it is required to define if a specific broadcaster will send the emergency alert or involve multiple broadcasters, which affects the type of receiver used. For this reason, the proposal of the present work is the adaptation of an EWBS signal taken from a set-top box to an IP Telephony Server that forwards or replicates the emergency alert in order to give the EWBS signal more excellent utility and better use.

One of the options of devices for the detection and emission of the EWBS signal is the IP telephone, which has a use in most companies and workspaces because the implementation of an IP telephony network has several advantages such as the simplification of infrastructure, advanced functions that can be developed employing software and additional services, which only this type of telephony can offer, so we based this work on the adaptation of an EWBS signal taken from a receiver (decoder) to an IP Telephony Server, thus giving the EWBS

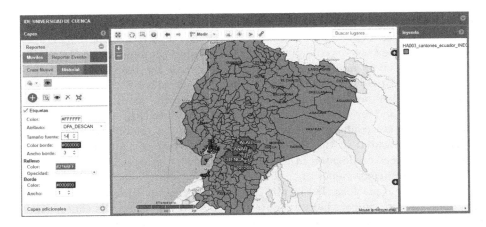

Fig. 1. EWBS code generator system of the SDI UCuenca

signal a more excellent utility and better use. For the project's development, the IP Telephony Network (managed by CISCO servers), of the University Campus of the University of the Armed Forces - ESPE, was used as a test scenario.

2   Methodology

For the project's development, the IP Telephony Network of the University Campus of the University of the Armed Forces ESPE was used as a test scenario. For the IP telephony system with signals coming from the outside as it is the warning emergency alert EWBS, the reason why we saw ourselves in the necessity to look for a way to make this integration, finding that most optimal, was to use a server of telephony IP like Asterisk since the programming language Python supports libraries coming from this Server. In this way, once an EWBS signal is detected under Python programming, the same program is responsible for transmitting the emergency signal through a kind of "call" from the Asterisk Server to the University Server.

For the development of this work, the following tools were used:

– Raspberry Pi 3 Model b+.
– Raspbian Buster with desktop and recommended software.
– Python version 3.7.3.
– Asterisk version 15.7.3.
– PIX-BT108-LA1 decoder from Pixela Corporation.

2.1   IP Telephony Server Under the Asterisk platform.-

For the installation of the server, initially, the Raspbian Operating System was updated, and all the necessary libraries for the Asterisk VPS (Virtual Private Server) were installed. After that, we proceeded to download and install Asterisk in version 15.7.3.

The operation of Asterisk is handled under the configuration of plain text files, so two files were modified, which were: sip.conf, because it contains the instructions for interaction with VoIP devices operating under the SIP protocol, and extensions.conf, it contains the configuration of phones, voice mailboxes, dialing plan, among others.

Plain Text File SIP.conf.- In the sip.conf file, we add the configuration of two users called [8640] and [TRUNK-CISCO]. The user [8640] was configured to execute tests of the correct functioning of the PBX in terms of incoming and outgoing calls. User [TRUNK-CISCO] was configured on the Asterisk PBX as a provider from the CISCO PBX. This user is used to carry out communication tests between the Asterisk Central and the CISCO Central. The configuration parameters are presented below, and the values used of both users in the Asterisk Central are shown in Table 1.

- type: Taking the friend of the value for the case of the user [8640], since this allows receiving and making calls internally in the Asterisk server, and peer for the case of the user [TRUNK-CISCO] since this only allows the authentication of outgoing calls.
- secret: If Asterisk is acting as a SIP Server, then this SIP client must login with an Authentication Password.
- qualify: Check if the client is reachable. Checks, in this case, are performed with a latency time of less than 2000 ms.
- port: UDP port on which the Asterisk Central will respond.
- insecure: Defines how to handle connections when the type parameter is set to peers.
- nat: This variable changes Asterisk's behavior for clients behind a firewall.
- host: This parameter is used to define how to find the client. The dynamic value serves to allow the user to connect from any IP address on the network.
- careinvite: This parameter indicates if the client can support SIP re-invite. The default value is yes.
- disallow: Allows to disable or enable a codec. The default value is all.
- allaw: Allows the use of codecs in order of preference. Usually, you must always define first the disallow parameter with the value all.
- context: This parameter depends on the value defined in the type parameter. In the case of the project, that value is friend, so this context is based on the calls that enter or leave through the definition of SIP entities.

Plain Text File Extensions.conf.- In the extensions.conf file, we proceeded to declare the configuration for three numbers, the first being the Central's own in Asterisk, which was generated for testing. The second number is for the CISCO IP central of the University; this and the first number were also generated with the purpose of testing. The third number is the access code to the INFORMACAST of the CISCO IP Exchange of the University. This number

Table 1. User settings [8640] and [TRUNK-CISCO], in the sip.conf plain text file.

	[8640]	[TRUNK-CISCO]
Type	Friend	Peer
Secret	8640pass	Does not apply
Qualify	Yes	Yes
Port	Does not apply	5060
Insecure	Does not apply	Port invite
Nat	No	No
Host	Dynamic	IP of the CISCO Central
Canreinvite	No	All
Disallow	All	All
Allaw	Ulaw, Alaw	Ulaw, Alaw
Context	Public	Public

contains all the extensions of the University, in which at the moment that the EWBS signal is detected, the speaker of these extensions will be automatically activated. It is a mass emergency notification system that sends critical messages to local devices and mobile users belonging to an IP telephony network and can also send to other types of receivers or social networks, as shown in Fig. 2.

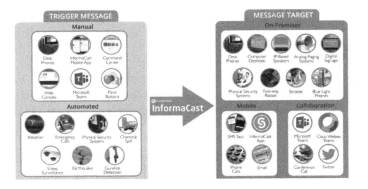

Fig. 2. INFORMACAST

Table 2 shows the configuration of the 3 numbers configured in the extensions.conf file.

2.2   EWBS Signal Detection

The designed receiver tests were conducted with controlled transmission broadcast in the laboratory. An ISDB-T Dektec DTU-215 modulator was used for the RF output and the EWBS server with the transport flow configuration presented

Table 2. Configuration of the numbers in the plain text file extensions.conf. Each number must have a line under the parameter (Dial), to establish a new outgoing connection on a channel, and then link it to the incoming channel of the call; and a line under the parameter (Hangup), to end the call.

	General context
exten	8640, 1, Dial(SIP/8640, 30, Ttm)
exten	8640, 2, Hangup
exten	1874, n, Dial(SIP/TRUNK-CISCO/${EXTEN})
exten	1874, n, Hangup
exten	7400, n, Dial(SIP/TRUNK-CISCO/${EXTEN})
exten	7400, n, Hangup

in Table 3, with different area codes of Ecuador based on the harmonization document. Part 3 of the Forum ISDB-T International [6].

Table 3. Transmitter configuration

Paramenters	Values	
Program Map Table (PMT)	PID: 1031	
Program number	59232	
Emergency information descriptor	$0 \times FC$	
Country code (ecuador)	0×454355	
Area codes	Quito	$168, 0 \times A8$
	Rumiñahui	$172, 0 \times AC$
	Mejía	$108, \times 6C$
	Latacunga	$97, 0 \times 61$
	Pujilí	$159, 0 \times 9F$
	Salcedo	$173, 0 \times AD$
	Ambato	$5, 0 \times 05$
Superimpose message in spanish	*"Alerta, evacuar el edificio"*	
PID message	278	

To integrate the EWBS signal to the IP Telephony Server, a PIXELA decoder receives the EWBS signal and activates an audible alarm according to the emergency code. The Raspberry card was used to monitor and capture the electronic signal that activates the alarm through a function implemented in Python. For the programming, we proceeded to perform the detection of the event (1 or 0 logical) coming from the decoder, followed by this, through the import of the *pycall* library, which is compatible with all the attributes of Asterisk call files, it was declared that at the moment the program detects a one logical automatically connects with the Asterisk server to initiate a call to the number designated for the INFORMACAST belonging to the CISCO Central.

2.3   Integration and Testing

In Fig. 3, can see the interconnection diagram between the interface and the network of the University of the Armed Forces ESPE, in which the first one has a CUCM Publisher module, which allows the reading and writing of the platform's database, where all the changes are made, that is to say, user declarations, extensions, among others. Furthermore, the second one has a CUCM Subscriber module, which only allows reading and saving the information that the Publisher replicates to the other subscribers of the solution and an INFORMACAST module. When the EWBS console emits a message, the system works as follows: it triggers an electrical pulse in the decoder, which the Raspberry detects through programming in Python. Once the detection process is done, the program in Python called detect.py calls the number 7400, which is the code assigned in the INFORMACAST, to activate the Speakers of the University's phones automatically.

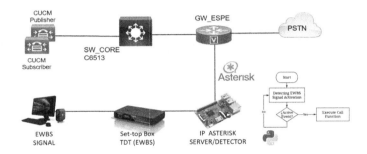

Fig. 3. Interconnection diagram between the interface and the IP network

In this scenario, what was finally executed was that, at the time of detecting the activation pin of the decoder, make the call to a number previously configured within the INFORMACAST of the Central CISCO, so that the speakers of the IP terminals of the Central are activated automatically emitting the signal of Emergency through audio.

Figure 4 represents the full implementation of the work, after that detecting the activation pin of the decoder, make the call to a number previously configured within the INFORMACAST of the Central CISCO so that the speakers of the IP terminals of the Central are activated automatically emitting the signal of Emergency employing audio.

2.4   Test Scenarios

To obtain the results, four test scenarios were performed. The first test scenario was implemented exclusively to validate the detection of the decoder's electric pulse under Python programming on the Raspberry, which in this case acted only as a detector once it received the EWBS signal from the Console.

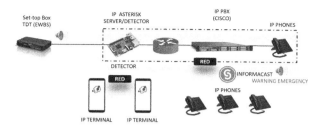

Fig. 4. Total work implementation diagram.

Figure 5 shows the implementation of scenario 1, in which once the detector identifies an electric pulse equal to 1.6 V, the time and day in which the electric pulse was detected is presented in the interface through a command window.

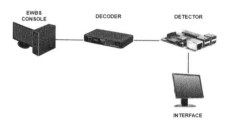

Fig. 5. Test scenario no. 1.

Scenario 2 was performed to test the operation of the Asterisk PBX implemented on the Raspberry after its installation.

The tests consisted initially of communicating two telephones previously registered in the PBX to determine that there are no errors in communication in the IP telephony system.

Following this, the detection system used in Scenario 1 was incorporated so that, instead of visualizing the detection through a command window, the detection is visualized through a telephone call to the IP Terminal. Figure 6 shows this scenario in Phase 2.

Scenario 3 was performed in 2 phases shown in Figs. 7 and 8, respectively. The first one, to execute communication tests between the Asterisk IP PBX and the CISCO IP PBX. When calling from extension 8640 (belonging to the Asterisk PBX) to extension 1874 (belonging to the CISCO PBX), successful communication was achieved due to the configuration of the Asterisk user as a friend type within the Asterisk PBX in which it was determined that it could make calls.

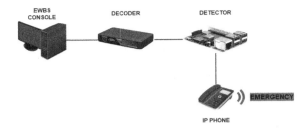

Fig. 6. Test scenario no. 2.

When calling from extension 1874 to extension 8640, no communication was obtained because the CISCO user configuration within the Asterisk PBX was defined as a peer, allowing the CISCO PBX to receive calls.

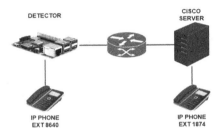

Fig. 7. Test scenario no. 3 (phase 1).

In the second phase, the call was made directly from the Asterisk Central to extension 1874, once the Raspberry detected the high pulse when the decoder obtained the EWBS signal coming from the Console.

In scenario 4 is shown in Figs. 9, when the decoder activation pin was detected, the call to a number previously configured within the INFORMACAST of the CISCO Central Station was automatically executed so that the speakers of the IP terminals of the Central Station were automatically activated, emitting the Emergency signal employing audio.

3   Results

The transmission was made from the laboratory ISDB-T transmitter through broadcast on channel 30 UHF at a transmission frequency of 569.143 MHz, activated the transport stream with the configuration for EWBS described in Table 3.

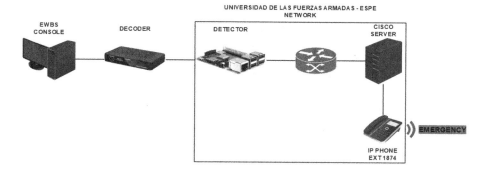

Fig. 8. Test scenario no. 3 (phase 2).

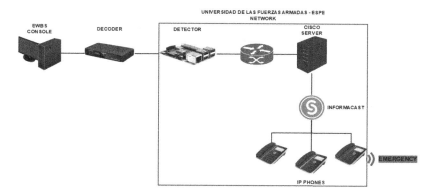

Fig. 9. Test scenario no. 4.

Three different city codes were evaluated with ten consecutive tests for each one. One hundred percent detection of the activated electrical pulse was obtained once the decoder received the EWBS signal. There were no false positives in any of the tests, which allowed us to ensure that there would be no false alarms in the operation process.

The IP Terminal was automatically called when the detector obtained the active electrical pulse once the EWBS signal was emitted. Since the detector's sampling time was 1 s in the programming, while the electric pulse was high, calls were made every 1 s, which allowed us to define a sampling time of 30 s.

When calling from an extension belonging to the Asterisk Central to an extension belonging to the CISCO Central, successful communication was achieved due to the configuration of the Asterisk user as a friend within the Asterisk Central in which it was determined that it could make calls.

INFORMACAST replied to the emergency alert through audio messages to both fixed and portable telephones of the Asterisk central and the CISCO central.

With the results obtained, it was possible to validate that there are no delays in the reception of the emergency alert in the IP Telephony network. As soon as the EWBS signal is activated, the speakers of the IP terminals are automatically activated, emitting the pre-recorded alert message.

The tests can be seen in: https://youtu.be/QWw8UaWGRQQ.

4   Discussion

To implement the EWBS system is necessary to define the complete structure of its transmission system through Digital Terrestrial Television under the ISDB-T standard, so it was essential first to develop a server that inserts the codes of each of the cantons of the country and the superimpose message that will be sent for the emergency alert in the transport stream of the television channel that is structured on the programming sent. In addition, a system was designed that allows the control of the emergency terminal to work in a centralized way to activate the signal to the television channel stations remotely.

Field tests were carried out in the city of Quito through a single television station, but the question of implementation remains since the EWBS system will only work when it is tuned to this channel or if it is on Standby. Some receivers receive the signal by tuning to a specific channel for Standby mode, making it dependent on a single television channel. For the possibility of increasing the emergency alert to the entire population, it would be if all the television channels that have digital transmission activate the EWBS system, which makes the centralized control send to several stations and not necessarily the entire population receives this signal.

On the receiving side, it is essential, on the one hand, that digital television receivers with the EWBS emergency alert system for the international ISDB-T standard should enter the market of each country and, on the other hand, that they also have audible alarms, text superimposes message and the standby output support, which affects all televisions and receivers that have entered the country since 2014 with the international ISDB-T standard that do not necessarily have the EWBS system.

To start the process of implementing the EWBS system in the country that supports coverage and reaches the entire population is necessary to find a way to take advantage of technology, thinking differently, giving support to a few television stations in the country destined to send the emergency alert that they have a centralized system that includes a backup and redundancy network, operating under an international communication protocol.

It is important to take advantage of the broadcast television signal coverage throughout the country to send the emergency alert and not necessarily receive it on the television and have reception equipment tuned to the television channel in charge of EWBS that retransmits that information, be it in the form through communal alarms on speakers, or through internal or external networks, either through the Internet or other means of communication.

In this article, we present the option of taking advantage of receivers already available in the market with the EWBS system, which replicates the emergency signal in an internal network through a telephone exchange, for which a telephone exchange was designed through a Raspberry Pi card IP that was connected to a corporate telephone exchange, in this case of the university, which allows that through its massive information system INFORMACAST, it can replicate all the telephones contacted to the corporate center and also to the individual central.

Similar projects have been developed for communal speakers through the cooperation of JICA and INICTEL of Peru using a specialized chip for receiving EWBS in one segment, which has proven to be a good solution for coastal areas that warn of Tsunami emergencies, which to at the same time it includes an audio message that comes out of the speakers, all sent through the television signal.

The tests we carry out on our prototype consider that we control the transmission and reception process, so the text message is sent to both a television receiver and is the same as the one sent by the telephone exchange. However, when conducting field tests through television channels, the EWBS receiver will continue to present the message sent over the television. However, the IP control panel will only receive the emergency activation, so the development of complete receivers that fulfill the role of Gateway has continued. We have developed a second phase based on a receiver designed with Software Defined Radio (SDR) that thoroughly reads the transport stream and can also detect the activation of the emergency message through the physical layer and decode the area codes and the message from text transmitted over the air, as well as the possibility of sending the replica of all this information to the network.

Acknowledgments. This project internal financing from the Research Directorate of the University of Cuenca and the *Universidad de las Fuerzas Armadas* ESPE PIJ-07.

References

1. Shogen, K., Ito, Y., Hamazumi, H., Taguchi, M.: Implementation of emergency warning broadcasting system in the Asia Pacific region. In: ITU/ESCAP Disaster Communications Workshop, Bangkok, Thailand (2006)
2. V. Costales, F.: A 9 días de ocurrido el terremoto, 655 personas fallecieron y 48 están desaparecidas. Diario EL COMERCIO, (2016)
3. Instituto Geofísico EPN: Cotopaxi. https://www.igepn.edu.ec/cotopaxi. Accessed 17 Apr 2019
4. Atacuri D.: Experiencia del Perú en el desarrollo de un prototipo Instituto Nacional de Investigación y Capacitación en Telecomunicaciones en EWBS. ITU (2017). https://www.itu.int/en/ITU-D/Emergency-Telecommunications/SiteAssets/Pages/Events/2016/Ecuador-2017/EWBS
5. Olmedo, G., Acosta, F., Haro, R., Villamarín, D., Benavides, N.: Broadcast testing of emergency alert system for digital terrestrial television EWBS in ecuador. In: Abásolo, M.J., Silva, T., González, N.D. (eds.) jAUTI 2018. CCIS, vol. 1004, pp. 176–187. Springer, Cham (2019). https://doi.org/10.1007/978-3-030-23862-9_13
6. DiBEG.: ISDB-T Harmonization Documents Part 3 EWBS. (2015). https://www.dibeg.org/techp/aribstd/harmonization.html

7. ARIB: Data Multiplex Broadcasting System for the Conventional Television Using the Sound Sub Carrier. ARIB STD-B14 (1998). https://www.arib.or.jp/english/std_tr/broadcasting/std-b14.html

8. Olmedo, G., Acosta, F., Villamarín, D., Santander, F., Achig, R., Morocho, V.: Prototype of a centralized alert and emergency system for digital terrestrial television in ecuador. In: Botto-Tobar, M., Cruz, H., Díaz Cadena, A. (eds.) CIT 2020. AISC, vol. 1326, pp. 191–201. Springer, Cham (2021). https://doi.org/10.1007/978-3-030-68080-0_14

9. OASIS: Common Alerting Protocol (2010). http://docs.oasis-open.org/emergency/cap/v1.2/CAP-v1.2.html

10. Eliot, C: Protocolo Común de Alerta (CAP) (2018). https://etrp.wmo.int/pluginfile.php/16534/mod_resource/content/1/2018-MISC-WDS-CAP-Protocol-Comun-18856_es.pdf

11. Morocho, V., Achig, R., Santander, F., Bautista, S.: Spatial data infrastructure as the core for activating early alerts using EWBS and interactive applications in digital terrestrial television. In: Rocha, Á., Ferrás, C., Paredes, M. (eds.) ICITS 2019. AISC, vol. 918, pp. 346–355. Springer, Cham (2019). https://doi.org/10.1007/978-3-030-11890-7_34

New Solution for the Packaging and Delivery the Interactive Services of the Cuban Terrestrial Digital Television

Juan Carlos González Fernández, Joaquín Pina Amargós[✉][iD], Raisa Socorro Llanes[iD], and David Paredes Miranda

Universidad Tecnológica de La Habana "José Antonio Echeverría" (CUJAE), Havana, Cuba
{jpina,dparedes,raisa}@ceis.cujae.edu.cu
http://cujae.edu.cu/comunidad/jpina

Abstract. The interactive services of Cuban Terrestrial Digital Television (TDT) offer useful information to viewers. Currently, the processes that ensure the operation of interactive services in Cuba require a complex and expensive hardware infrastructure. In addition, the service provider has the obligation to pay licenses for the use of proprietary software that limits its modification to adapt it to the real needs. A new solution is presented in this paper, that obtains the interactivity data packages them according to the defined standard and delivers the TS following two methods: by IP/UDP and by means of a modulation device. The complete process was tested at the laboratory level and its proper functioning was verified in several available STBs and in the analysis of the formed TS following the standard. The software called PaqTVC+ is multiplatform, sovereign and requires few resources for its operation so it can be used as a practical tool in Cuban TDT and opens up new possibilities for its development.

Keywords: Terrestrial digital television · Interactive services · Packaging

1 Introduction

Digital terrestrial television (DTT) is a digital transmission system that takes advantage of the distribution network of analog terrestrial television. It can be received by means of the same antennas with a small cost of adaptation, this allows a faster and less expensive migration to digitization. The use of this technology makes it possible to broadcast more television channels with greater definition and includes the new interactive services [2,10].

Supported by Perez-Guerrero Trust Fund for South-South Cooperation (PGTF) United Nations Development Programme (UNDP) project INT/19/K08 and Ministry of Communications of Cuba.

© Springer Nature Switzerland AG 2021
M. J. Abásolo et al. (Eds.): jAUTI 2020, CCIS 1433, pp. 45–57, 2021.
https://doi.org/10.1007/978-3-030-81996-5_4

Cuba is immersed in the transition to digital television. In 2011, an agreement was signed between the National Development and Reform Commission of the people's Republic of China and the current Ministry of Communications of the Republic of Cuba, for the adoption by Cuba of the Digital Terrestrial Multimedia Broadcasting standard (DMB-T or also known as DTMB). The technical specifications were subsequently published in 2015 [11]. The agreement included a donation of equipment, technology and technical advice to begin the transition [14].

Interactive services are in the general flow of Cuban DTT, complementing the television and radio signal. These offer viewers additional and useful information such as: the electronic programming guide (EPG). In addition, through the Data Broadcasting Service different contents are transmitted such as: news, the weather forecast in Cuba, among others. The contents of this service are collected the weather forecast in Cuba, among others. The contents of this service are collected from the primary news sources and delivered by the TVC+ software to the data server with a high frequency of updating of the information [12].

There are different systems that implement DTT interactive services processes such as those based on the standard [6]. In the case of the data broadcasting service, these softwares have been donated by the Chinese company *Compunicate Technologies Inc.* [7]. However, the implementations of these systems do not easily adapt to the current development of DTT and do not follow the country's policy of promoting the development of Free and Open-source Software (FOSS), needing the Windows platform for its operation and the payment of its respective license (see Fig. 1).

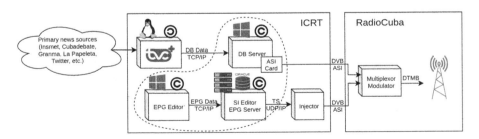

Fig. 1. Simplified diagram of processes that ensure the operation of interactive services in Cuba. Complex, proprietary and expensive equipment and software appear enclosed within the dotted line.

In addition, the deployment of these systems involves the use of several expensive servers, with an oversized architecture. Therefore, the current system for the packaging and delivery of the content of the interactive services of the DTT has a high complexity, technological dependence and difficulty of adaptation to new requirements, generating economic expenses to the country to maintain this infrastructure. This is of greater importance because of the conditions imposed by the genocidal blockade imposed by the United States Government against Cuba [15].

This paper presents an FOSS-based solution that allows the packaging and delivery of the content of the interactive services of the Cuban DTT.

2 Background of the Investigation

Currently, the Cuban DTT includes the programming guide and the Information Service of data broadcasting on which the development of this work is focused.

Interactive services obtain information from one or more entities known as a content provider. It obtains the content from primary sources, and then provides this information to the server or interactive servers (EPG and DB). The servers contain the systems for processing this content. These systems will structure the data that make up the services according to DVB and MPEG-2 standards. The generated TS, usually elementary transport flows, contain a single DTT service and are transmitted from the servers (EPG, DB and A/V) to the line head, where they are combined into a final TS that is modulated according to the DMB-T standard and is finally transmitted. Viewers receive the digital signal with antennas connected to DTT boxes, hybrid TVs or other devices.

The data broadcasting service is satisfied with information from primary sources of information such as: Radio Reloj, the Institute of Meteorology, and others. In the conformation and dissemination of this service are executed processes of selection and structuring of the information, packaging of the data and delivery of the content.

The selection and structuring is carried out by the TVC+ system [1,9,17] where the information files to be transmitted are generated. The generated files are stored in a TAR extension archiver. This file cabinet is accessed through a service provided by TVC+ itself. These files then go through the packaging process.

The services information introduces several tables to simplify the operations of the digital signal receivers [5]. These are: *network information table* (NIT), *Service Descriptor Table* (SDT), *Bouquet Association Table* (BAT), *Event Information Table* (EIT), *Running Status Table* (RST), *Time-Date Table* (TDT), *Time Offset Table* (TOT) y *Stuffing Table* (ST).

Packaging consists of writing information into MPEG-2 transport packages as defined in [8]. This process requires downloading and unpacking the information files produced by TVC+. This task is executed by TDT_TimerService, a system that acts as a bridge between the TVC+ and FDC_Services applications. FDC_Services is the system deployed on the data server and is responsible for the packaging and transmission of the information files. Deficiencies in communication between these parties sometimes result in the failure to transmit the latest available information.

In the case of EPG, there is an infrastructure composed of a server to process and deliver the service to a specialized device called Injector whose function is the transformation of the IP flow into an ASI signal; it is appreciated, once again, the complexity and technological dependence of the current architecture (see Fig. 1).

The files necessary to make up the EPG are generated by a system developed by the Cuban company DeSoft. These files are copied and moved on a USB device to the EpgEditor application deployed on the EPG server. The files contain the events or programs in the guide and their descriptions. This content is processed by the EPG server that generates a TS with the NIT, SDT, EIT; TDT and TOT tables and is transmitted to the Injector, then delivered to the line head.

Table 1. Current infrastructure for packaging and delivery of interactive services.

Components	Data services	EPG
Servers	1	1
Platform	Windows	Windows
Specialized hardware	ASI card	Injector

The final process is the delivery of the TS to the line head. In this process the TS generated in the packaging is delivered by means of an ASI signal that carries the binary flow of the TS to the multiplexer in the case of both interactivity services. Each TS delivered by the interactivity servers with the information of the services, reaches the multiplexer. It produces a TS with the multiplexed contents of all Cuban DTT services. This TS is modulated to DTMB and sent to the dissimilar devices that perform the final transmission to the air. Table 1 shows a summary of the complexity and dependence of the infrastructure of the interactive services of the Cuban DTT.

3   Proposed Solution: PaqTVC+

The solution presented in this paper consists of a system that allows the processing of interactive DTT services. The proposal is not an isolated system, it has to communicate with the systems that collect the information and generate the files necessary for the processing of interactivity services. The new software was named PaqTVC+ considering that it packages the information generated by TVC+. The input files that will be processed and delivered by PaqTVC+ will be archived in a TAR archiver without compression or encryption for each service. The Fig. 2 illustrates the simplification of the process that will ensure the operation of interactive services in Cuba. The above contrasts with the current process shown in the Fig. 1. As currently delivered in the case of the data broadcasting service. These archivers must be available to be downloaded by the application through the use of REST services.

In the case of the archiver for the data broadcasting service, the information files will contain the contents of the service in the following formats: XML files for the description of news, sections and other data of interest, images files to be included and MPEG of video files.

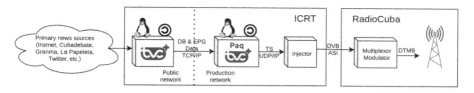

Fig. 2. Simplified diagram of the proposed new process that ensures the operation of interactive services in Cuba.

```
<?xml version="1.0" encoding="UTF-8"?>
  <ProviderInfo id="ICRT IS-EPG">
   <SchedulerData type="program" language_code="spa" program_name ="Cubavision">
    <event event_id="1" start_time="2020-08-20 09:00:00" duration="02:00:00" CA_mode="true">
      <short_event_descriptor language_code="eng">
        <event_name>Evento de prueba</event_name>
        <text>Evento con todos los descriptores soportados.</text>
      </short_event_descriptor>
     <content_descriptor>
       <content content_nibble_level_1="0x9" content_nibble_level_2="0x2" user_byte="0x00"/>
     </content_descriptor>
     <extended_event_descriptor descriptor_number="0x01" last_descriptor_number="0x01" language_code="eng">
       <text>Descripcion detallada de un evento en adicion al short event descriptor.</text>
       <item><description>Descripcion item</description> <name>Texto item</name> </item>
     </extended_event_descriptor>
     <CA_identifier_descriptor> <CA_system_id value="0x0001"/> </CA_identifier_descriptor>
    </event>
    <event event_id="2" start_time="2020-08-20 11:00:00" duration="00:30:00" CA_mode="false">
      <time_shifted_event_descriptor reference_service_id="0x0001" reference_event_id="0x0001"/>
    </event>
   </SchedulerData>
  </ProviderInfo>
```

(a) For EPG events

```
<?xml version="1.0" encoding="UTF-8"?>
<ProviderInfo id="ICRT IS-EPG" data="Service Descriptor Table" data_last_modification="2020-08-04 8:00:00" network_name="NOMBRE_RED" network_id="100">
 <SDT version="1" transport_stream_id="1" original_network_id="100" >
  <service service_id="1" EIT_schedule="true" EIT_present_following="true" CA_mode="false">
    <service_descriptor service_type="0x01" service_provider_name="Radiocuba" service_name="Cubavision"/>
  </service>
 </SDT>
 <SDT version="1" transport_stream_id="0" original_network_id="1" >
  <service service_id="19" EIT_schedule="true" EIT_present_following="true" CA_mode="false" >
    <service_descriptor service_type="0x01" service_provider_name="Radiocuba" service_name="HD1"/>
  </service>
 </SDT>
</ProviderInfo>
```

(b) For synchronization of services and network information

Fig. 3. Part of the input XML files

In the case of the archiver for the EPG interactive service, the information files must be in XML format. They will contain the information of the events or programs that will be broadcast on Cuban DTT channels (Cubavisión, TeleRebelde, etc.) in addition to the name file (si_sdt.xml) that will allow the synchronization of the information of the SI that is generated in an external system. The synchronization of this information allows consistency in it for all components of the DTT network and is a requirement raised by the customer. In the EPG archiver there will be one XML file per channel. The specific structure designed for the EPG information files is seen in Fig. 3(a). The file si_sdt.xml is a model designed to facilitate understanding between the systems involved in the processing of SI information and follows the structure presented in the Fig. 3(b).

Currently the information provided from events or programs is very limited. The new solution includes the possibility of transmitting more than one descriptor for the EPG which, in case of taking advantage of this feature, enriches the data that is presented to the viewer. For example, using the content_descriptor allows you to specify the type of content being viewed; be it a series, Movie, News, among many other categories and subcategories that are defined in the standard in [3].

4 TSDuck: Packaging and Delivery of Services

TSDuck [16] is an extensible toolkit for MPEG transport streams. It is used in digital television systems for test, monitoring, integration, debug, lab, etc. TSDuck contains a number of useful tools for processing TS, of which, transport stream processor (TSP) is the main one. TSP is a framework for working with TS. In general TSP uses an input plugin to load a TS. This is processed using different plugins for packet processing, at the programmer's choice and finally uses an output plugin to obtain the results of the processing performed. All plugins used by tsp are libraries (.so files on Linux and .dll on Windows). The tools provided by TSDuck can be used through commands on both operating systems and this is the case with TSP and the different plugins.

TSP plugins in combination with the class design of the solution allow the processing of the contents of interactivity services; producing TS files as a result of the packaging of such services. Upon completion of the processing of the interactive EPG and Data Broadcasting Services, various files stored in the application resource directory are obtained. At the end of this process you get two TS one for each service. In the TS of the EPG are also the PIDS containing the NIT, SDT and EIT tables, while in TS of the data broadcasting service are the PIDs with the information of the BAT and FDT (File Description Table) tables.

Delivering the content of interactive services to the head of line is the ultimate goal of PaqTVC+ and one of the most important processes. There are two modes of transmission that have been presented as a requirement for this process: transmission over UDP/IP and transmission to a DekTec device that modulates the final TS. In both cases the transmission process begins right after the processing of the content of the interactive services is completed. Your first task is to create a transmission buffer that is nothing more than a TS with the set of all services and data processed. It includes the TOT and DTT tables that contain the date, local time and the information corresponding to the current time zone.

Delivery via a standard route such as UDP/IP simplifies the complexity of the current system and offers a versatile way to deliver interactivity data. While in laboratory conditions, modulation by DekTec devices is very useful to have a fast and effective way to visualize the result of the processing of the new software developed PaqTVC+. In this case, the infrastructure and equipment needed to quickly check how the receivers react to the transmitted content is reduced.

The new software solution proposal was designed following four fundamental goals: to be based on free software, which could work on Linux and Windows platforms, reduce dependence on specialized hardware and require few computing resources for its operation. At the same time, the solution must ensure the essential processes required for the interactive services of the Cuban DTT.

As seen in Table 2 the solution does not require large hardware power to develop its tasks; common computers are sufficient for its operation. The developed system requirements make it possible to use it as a common software tool, without excessive restrictions and which can perform advanced tasks in a simple laboratory environment.

Table 2. Requirements for the use of the new software PaqTVC+

Parameters	Minimum requirements	Recommended requirements
Operation system (SO)	Windows 10 or Linux 18.04	Windows 10 or Linux 18.04
Processor	Intel Dual Core 1.7 GHz	Intel Core i3 1.7 GHz or higher
RAM	2 GB	4 GB
Storage	500 MB	1 GB
Connectivity	LAN card and USB	LAN card and USB
TSDuck version	3.19–1520	3.19–1520 or higher

5   Discussion

In the world, directly analyzing the TS has become the most important test method for DTT. At each site where DTT is transmitted the TS are analyzed and monitored by MPEG-2 TS decoders.

MPEG-2 TS analysis is a special type of logical analysis. The errors that can be detected are divided into three types according to their priority: type 1, 2 and 3 as summarized in the Table 2. If there are Type 1 errors it is often not possible to decode the programs; the presence of Type 2 errors, on the other hand, means that partially there is no possibility to play a program correctly. The presence of Type 3 errors indicates errors in the transmission of SI information and their effects depend on how the receivers (decoder boxes, hybrid TVs, etc.) react to them [4].

The Fig. 4 shows the analysis of a TS generated by the new proposed solution, where there is an absence of continuity errors and duplicate packages. This proves the compliance of the new solution with the DVB standard in the packaging of interactivity data (Table 3).

Table 3. Types of errors in the analysis of MPEG-2 TS.

Type 1 errors	Type 2 errors	Type 3 errors
TS sync loss	Transport error	SI repetition error
Sync byte error	CRC error	NIT error
PAT error	PCR error	SDT error
PMT error	PCR accuracy error	EIT error
Continuity count error	PTS error	RST error
PID error	CAT error	TDT error
		Undefined PID

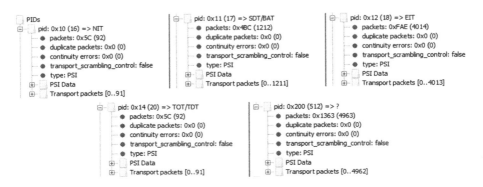

Fig. 4. Portions of DVB Inspector screens where it is observed that there are no errors in the TS generated by PaqTVC+

The visualization of the information from the interactivity data is another effective test for new solution managing to show the additional content to the viewers on their TVs. With this intention, the modulation functionality implemented by the new software using the DekTec DTU-215 device was tested following the scheme shown in the Fig. 5.

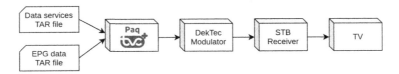

Fig. 5. Flowchart of the complete process using PaqTVC+, which includes: packaging of interactivity data from TAR files, packaging and delivery to the modulator, modulation, reception on an STB and viewing on an ordinary TV.

In this way, the software communicates with the device that is connected to a decoder box and this to the TV; and allowing to consult the interactivity services transmitted, as shown in the Fig. 6.

Fig. 6. Testing scenario.

The inclusion of modified data to demonstrate the correct functioning of the system will provide us with information related to this project. Thus the processing of the information of the interactive services could be completed and after the modulation of the generated TS it is possible to access the interactive services on the TV. The usual Information sections for the data broadcasting service are displayed and in the case of the services section a table with data related to the PaqTVC+ software is observed; therefore, the relationship with this work is checked, as shown in the Fig. 7(a). The rest of the headlines have been randomly accessed in all sections without presenting difficulties.

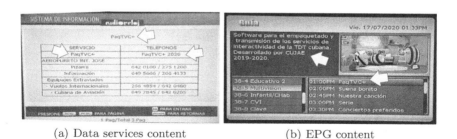

(a) Data services content   (b) EPG content

Fig. 7. Photographs of TV screens with the results where the changes of content is indicated with white arrows.

In the case of the EPG information, the events of the programming of the 8 standard definition channels (SD) of the Cuban DTT in the period from July 17 to 23, 2020 are observed. An event has been modified to display information about this work, as shown in the Fig. 7(b).

The following analysis of the UDP/IP transmission of the content of the interactive services seeks to demonstrate the correct functioning of this feature in the PaqTVC+ software. This test seeks to evaluate the packets transmitted over the network using this software and the correspondence of the same with the exclusive transmission of interactive services, maintaining a correct structure according to the MPEG-2 standard for TS.

Two computers connected via a LAN (PC-1 and PC-2) were used to perform this test. In the PC-1 you have the archivers (TAR) to be processed and the PaqTVC+ software through which the processing and transmission of the contents of the interactive services will be carried out. The PC-2 will function as a transmission receiver with WireShark software [13]. WireShark is used as a sniffer to analyze traffic generated on the network. This software is able to analyze TS and the different tables of the PSI/SI and its content; with this feature the correspondence between the transmitted and the received information will be evaluated once again.

The Figs. 8(a) and 8(b) show the BAT and EIT tables for the data broadcasting service and EPG that is packaged and transmitted from PC-1 to PC-2. As expected for this scenario a BAT with a single section was obtained to access the contents that were processed from the archive file (TAR) for the data broadcasting service.

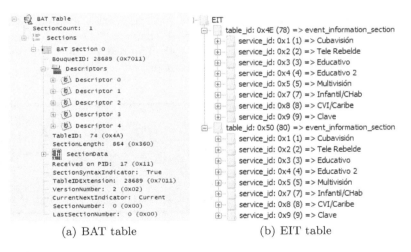

(a) BAT table   (b) EIT table

Fig. 8. Parts of DVB Inspector screens where tables of the TS generated by PaqTVC+ are observed.

These contents are 263 files (XML content files, BMP images and a video for the background in MPEG-2 format), which the system was expected to package a single section of the BAT and 5 descriptors as shown in Fig. 8(a). On the EIT table of the EPG can be seen in Fig. 8(b) that the present/following information is found in the table_id x4E and the itinerary in the table_id x50 of the 8 SD channels of the Cuban DTT. This information represents the events or programs in transmission and the programming for the given period of days of the channels, respectively.

(a) NIT table (b) NIT services

(c) SDT services (d) BAT table

(e) TOT table

Fig. 9. Parts of screens taken from the WireShark software that display the contents of the TS file received on the PC-2.

On the other hand, the Fig. 9(a) shows the NIT that has been captured using the WireShark software in the PC-2, where parameters such as: identifier, name and TS belonging to the current DTT network are highlighted; these parameters correspond to those currently used for the transmission of Cuban DTT. Figure 9(b) and Fig. 9(c) show the SD TV and radio services that are broadcast on the network. It can be observed that there is correspondence of the identifiers of the same both in the NIT (Fig. 9(b)) and in the SDT (Fig. 9(c)).

The Fig. 9(d) shows the BAT captured in this test and can be seen a correspondence between its structure and the analysis that was performed earlier and that is seen in Fig. 8(a). Five descriptors were obtained for the service: the first of them corresponds to the name of the bouquet (highlighted in yellow) and the other 4 to the linkage descriptors generated to reference the content of the service.

Finally, Fig. 9(e) shows the TOT corresponding to the time of transmission, which shows the date and time in UTC and the description of the next time zone change in Cuba. Images of the DTT and EIT were not included in this test, but correct behavior was observed in its content.

After completing this test, it is reaffirmed that the content packaged and delivered by the PaqTVC+ software corresponds to the information received through UDP/IP transmission; which includes, as expected, the NIT, SDT, BAT, TOT, DTT, EIT and FDT tables that contain the information necessary for the correct interpretation of the interactive services of the Cuban DTT.

6   Conclusions and Future Works

The main problems in the DTT process in Cuba are in the packaging of the data and delivery of the TS generated for transmission. In this work a solution was presented that obtains the interactivity data, packages them following the defined standard and delivers the TS both by UDP/IP and through a modulation device. The proposed system is multiplatform, based on free software and requires few resources for its operation. It can be used as a practical tool for the processing of Cuban DTT interactivity services and opens up new possibilities for their development. The interactive services information processed by the proposed system is received at the receivers in the expected manner. In this way it is possible to monitor the behavior of the different models of receivers before modifications in the design and presentation of the content of these services. As future works it remains to use TSDuck in the form of a library so that it is added the possibility of adapting its plugins to improve the experience of its use that allows it to be deployed in a production environment. As well as, reuse the current design of the solution for the data broadcasting service so that the classes involved in its processing can process other interactivity contents that make way for other interactive services for Cuban DTT.

Acknowledgements. This work was partially granted by Perez-Guerrero Trust Fund for South-South Cooperation, UNITED NATIONS, INT/19/*K08* "*Digital Terrestrial Television Applied to the Improvement of Developing Countries Peoples: Argentina, Brazil and Cuba*".

References

1. Amador-González, M.: Módulo para la extracción de información de fuentes externas para la conformación de noticias en la televisión digital en Cuba. Bachelor

thesis report Universidad Tecnológica de La Habana "José Antonio Echeverría" (CUJAE) (2018)

2. El-Hajjar, M., Hanzo, L.: A survey of digital television broadcast transmission techniques. IEEE Commun. Surv. Tutorials **15**(4), 1924–1949 (2013). https://doi. org/10.1109/SURV.2013.030713.00220

3. ETSI: Digital video broadcasting (DVB); signaling and carriage of interactive applications and services in hybrid broadcast/broadband environments. TS (102 809 V1.3.1) (2017)

4. Fischer, W.: Digital Video and Audio Broadcasting Technology: A Practical Engineering Guide. SCT. Springer, Heidelberg (2010). https://doi.org/10.1007/978-3-642-11612-4

5. Fischer, W.: Broadcast over internet, HbbTV, OTT, streaming. In: Fischer, W. (ed.) Digital Video and Audio Broadcasting Technology. SCT, pp. 903–913. Springer, Cham (2020). https://doi.org/10.1007/978-3-030-32185-7_44

6. HbbTV Association: Hybrid broadcast broadband TV HbbTV 2.0.1 Specif. HbbTV Association Res. Lib. (2019). https://www.hbbtv.org/resource-library

7. Compunicate Technologies INC: Official home page (2021). www.cti.com.cn/en/default.aspx

8. ITU, T.: Advanced video coding for generic audiovisual services. ITU-T Recommendation H. 264 (2003)

9. M., V.T., El.J., Castroand, R., Brito, R.M.L., Ríos, D.R.: Aplicación web para la gestión de los servicios de valor agregado de la televisión digital terrestre. Revista Telemática (3), 31–38 (2016)

10. Martínez Alonso, A., Martínez Alonso, R., Guillén Nieto, G.A.: Evaluación de parámetros de calidad seleccionados de cajas decodificadoras para el estándar DTMB. Ingeniería Electrónica, Automática y Comunicaciones **36**(2), 62–82 (2015)

11. Ministerio de las Comunicaciones de Cuba: Resolución no. 47/2015 que establece las especificaciones técnicas y de operación mínimas de la tv digital en el territorio nacional. Gaceta Oficial de la Rep. de Cuba No. 13, pp. 428–431 (2015)

12. Pina Amargós, J.D., Socorro Llanes, R., Paredes Miranda, D., Amador González, M., Villarroel Ramos, D.L.: Incorporation of immediacy, dynamics and interactivity to digital terrestrial television services in Cuba through TVC+. In: Abásolo, M.J., Kulesza, R., Pina Amargós, J.D. (eds.) jAUTI 2019. CCIS, vol. 1202, pp. 3–15. Springer, Cham (2020). https://doi.org/10.1007/978-3-030-56574-9_1

13. Sanders, C.: Practical Packet Analysis: Using Wireshark to Solve Real-world Network Problems. No Starch Press, San Francisco (2017)

14. Santana, Y.H., Betancourt, D.M., Valdes, A.I.M., Sanchez, Y.H., Nieto, G.A.G., Alonso, R.M.: DTMB monitoring tool based on a commercial set-top box. In: 2017 IEEE International Symposium on Broadband Multimedia Systems and Broadcasting (BMSB), pp. 1–6. IEEE (2017)

15. Secretary-General, U., et al.: Necessity of ending the economic, commercial and financial embargo imposed by the United States of America against Cuba. United Nations Digital Library (2020). https://digitallibrary.un.org/record/3889682?ln=en

16. TSDuck.io: MPEG Transport Stream Toolkit User's Guide (2021). https://tsduck.io/download/docs/tsduck.pdf

17. Villarroel-Ramos, D.L.: Módulo para la gestión del servicio de datos de la televisión digital en Cuba. Bachelor thesis report Universidad Tecnológica de La Habana "José Antonio Echeverría" (CUJAE) (2017)

iTV and Videos in Learning

Learning English with Second Screen Platforms: A Mixed Method Cross-National Study

Vagner Beserra[1]($\boxtimes$) ⓘ, Alan Angeluci[2] ⓘ, Alexandre Quaglio[2] ⓘ, and Carolina Falandes[2] ⓘ

[1] Universidad de Tarapacá, 18 de Septiembre 2222, Arica, Chile
[2] Universidade Municipal de São Caetano do Sul, Av. Goiás 3400, São Caetano do Sul, Brazil

Abstract. Contemporary world has set new stages of technology-driven transformations. Education calls special attention in this matter as digital environments are defining new forms to expand knowledge. Blended learning methods using multiple screens have emerged as new paradigms for facing recent new media appropriation and advancing the learning process in this digital scenario. A study was carried out with 59 students from the penultimate year of high school in Chile and Brazil to address this challenge. For two weeks, they participated in a flipped classroom for practicing basic English, experimenting with Digital Television and smartphone use. Results showed improvement of English skills among students comparing the pre and post-test periods. Also, it was observed that during the activity the students of both countries were mostly focused; however, the percentage of focused students decreased during the second half of the interaction period with the video in Digital Television inside the classroom. It should be mentioned that it was not the aim of this study to compare both countries, but to validate this strategy in two culturally different contexts. The study showed how practicing languages can be benefited with Digital Television use with multiple screens in flipped classrooms situations, being students affected by technology not only in the improvement of their learning but also because it opens opportunities to break down structures rooted in the teaching profession. Future works would be improved by conducting further sessions, amplifying the observation of students' content and characteristics.

Keywords: Teaching method · Learning environment · Multiple screens

1 Introduction

In the last decades, the socioeconomic, political, cultural, and technological transformations have significantly impacted individuals' lives. The appropriation of new media can be observed in work relations and, above all, in the education field, due to the rigidity of its structure [1]. According to Selwyn [2], digital technologies increasingly define education forms today since schools, universities, libraries, and museums have embraced digital artifacts, platforms, and applications, and it is impossible to imagine the future of a non-technology education. Thus, technological resources are progressively incorporated into the teaching-learning process as a way of mediation between

M. J. Abásolo et al. (Eds.): jAUTI 2020, CCIS 1433, pp. 61–76, 2021.
https://doi.org/10.1007/978-3-030-81996-5_5

the individual and knowledge, which helps in the formation and development of the citizen in the context in which it is inserted [3]. Morán [4] reports that there are no two worlds, physical and digital, when it comes to teaching and learning, but an extended space, an increased classroom, which can be merged and hybridized constantly. The COVID-19 pandemic strengthened the relevance of hybrid and active methodologies, stablishing the concatenation of physical and digital worlds the ultimate rule of living in a post-pandemic society.

In this perspective, teachers need to invest in new ways and methodologies of teaching centered in the students, to aid in the motivation and search for more autonomy [5]. In line with this thought, Beserra et al. [6] defend the creation of strategies that bring education and entertainment closer together, and different methods can be articulated to promote greater student engagement. To this end, one option to be considered is the so-called active methodologies, in which students centralize actions and construct knowledge collaboratively, unlike the traditional teaching method, focused on the transmission of knowledge by teachers [1]. Barbosa and Moura [7] corroborate this reasoning and add that in the active methods teachers act as mentors, supervisors, and facilitators since there is the intention to stimulate self-learning and to stimulate students' curiosity in researching solutions and building knowledge without receiving it passively.

Among the active methodologies, it is possible to highlight hybrid teaching, characterized by using technologies as the primary pedagogical resource. Bacich, Neto and de Melo Trevisani [8] affirm that this pedagogical approach presupposes a harmonious coexistence between face-to-face and distance activities, made through Information and Communication Technologies. A proposed hybrid methodology that has drawn attention in recent years is the flipped classroom, which according to Bergmann and Sams [9] can be summarized as "what is traditionally done in the classroom, now runs at home, and what is traditionally done at home, is now carried out in the classroom". Students receive the pedagogical resources of the subjects in advance and study at home; all possible questions or doubts are addressed before or during the lesson and following remedial practical activities with the teacher's assistance supervision. Bergmann [10] was able to observe in his searches a great preference of students for flipped homework assignments, since they can have a greater control of their learning, greater access to teachers and carry out studies in their own time. For Suhr [11], this method allows organizing the didactic activities in a more appropriate way to the student's needs, to reconcile the moments of self-learning with those of face-to-face interaction, regarding the rhythm of each student.

One of the resources used in the flipped classroom model is the audiovisual one. The audiovisual is increasingly present in education, but according to Divardin [12], predominantly in the context of linear learning, as schools do not seem to take advantage of the available technological resources, which diverges from the daily lives of young people and children, who progressively use cinema, television, digital games, the Internet, among other means of communication, to learn. From the perspective of Prata and Chambel [13], the video reveals itself as a tool that can enrich learning in different contexts when integrated with different devices and media. Talbert [14] considers that the cheapness, simplification, and greater access to online video recording and sharing technologies have made it easier to implement the flipped classroom. Also, the author sees in the application of this model a way to make the classroom more inclusive, active, and focused on the student, since it distances itself from a traditional classroom design, for an entire class, and is based on the assumptions of a personalized education.

Television, as well as other communication media at present, follow the dynamics of digitization, migrating from an analog system to a digital one, with superior image and sound quality, among other benefits. In Latin America, De Grande and Américo [15] show that several countries in the region chose to implement the Digital Terrestrial Transmission model. In 2006, Brazil was the first, while in Chile, the implantation started in 2009 with the same technology.

One of the main reasons for the effort to digitize TV is the growing need for inter-action between the user and television programming, pointed out as one of the main positive aspects of Digital Television, which currently divides the audience with other devices, such as smartphones and tablets, called "second screen". This competition has led television (first screen) to invest in complementary content for the user to access simultaneously through other screens, scenario that for Silva et al. [16] strengthens the need to identify solutions that seek a balance between the content of two or more screens to promote public attention.

Bringing the first and second screens to the educational field, since the new media are part of the daily practices of society, many possibilities of integration with the hybrid methodologies can be seen, like the flipped classroom, a model that still lacks further scientific contributions and improvements [17]. In this scenario, the present study, which employs a mixed, quantitative and qualitative approach, aims to measure the impact of the use of Digital Television with multiple screens during a flipped classroom to practice English.

2   Materials and Methods

A quasi-experimental exploratory study was carried out in two public schools: one in Brazil in the city of São Caetano do Sul, and another in Chile in the city of Arica - a total of 59 students, 4 girls and 30 boys (see Table 1); this gender distribution is typical in technical high schools in both countries. It should be mentioned that it was not the aim of this study to compare both schools, but rather, making the proposal of this work valid in two culturally different contexts. Also, considering the limitations of the project, some concerns were taken when selecting schools, for example, a similar number of courses, students, socioeconomic status of students, and representativeness in their contexts. Additionally, gender differences were not considered for data analysis, so the unbalanced gender count in both countries did not impact the scope analyzed.

The participants of both schools were students in their penultimate year of technical electrical high school, aged between 16 and 17 years old, who performed their regular activities in all disciplines, except for the English lessons, which is the subject of this work. For the content of the activities, English was chosen because it is a subject with a similar time load and syllabus/program at this level in both countries. Specifically, the contents related to personal presentation, tourist information, and the use of the verb to be in Simple Present.

The experiment was carried out over a period of two weeks, both in Chile and in Brazil, being structured from four sessions that followed the same protocols in both

Table 1. Class characteristics

Class	Brazil	Chile
Students per class	34	25
Participating students	27	17
Participating girls	3	1
Participating boys	24	16

countries: the first one lasting 60 min, and the other ones 90 min. In the first session, the 15 initial minutes were used to explain the research's objective to each group, and, in the remaining 45 min, the quantitative evaluation instrument (pre-test) described below was applied. At the end of the first session, three video classrooms were made available to the students (see Fig. 1). These video classrooms, lasting less than 10 min each, addressed the content to be learned, and students were instructed to watch at the time and place they consider suitable.

Fig. 1. Captures of content of the three video classrooms available to the students before the experimental work in the classroom.

In the second session, one week after the first, the first 10 min were used to install an application on the students' mobile devices (application described below). The remaining 80 min were focused on the activity itself; that is, clarify doubts and watch the interactive classroom video on Digital Television (see Fig. 2) and, through the mobile application on their devices, interact with the classroom video (both pedagogical tools described below). It is worth mentioning that the students at the end of the activity could continue working with the mobile application to practice the subjects depicted in the video classroom. In the third session, in the school and with the subject's teacher, the students eliminated their doubts and exercised the contents envisioned in the previous activity. For the exercise, the students could use the application in their mobiles or other material of their interest, always with the teacher's accompaniment. Finally, in the last session was divided into two parts; in the first, a quantitative evaluation (post-test) equivalent to the first (pre-test) was applied, that is, different but identical questions in number and level of difficulty. In the second part, a focus group was conducted to determine the degree of appreciation of the students with the set of activities. Figure 3 illustrates the flow of the sessions and their parts.

Fig. 2. Scenes from the interactive video presented in the classroom through Digital Television.

FIRST SESSION Duration: 60 minutes	- Initial 15 minutes: research explanation.
	- 45 minutes remaining: application of the quantitative evaluation instrument (pre-test).
	- Three video classrooms were made available to the students (to watch at a location of your choice within one week).
SECOND SESSION Duration: 90 minutes	- Initial 10 minutes: installing the application on students' mobile devices.
	- 80 minutes remaining: clarify doubts and watch the interactive classroom video on Digital Television and, through the mobile application, interact with the classroom video.
THIRD SESSION Duration: 90 minutes	- With the help of the subject's teacher, the students eliminated their doubts and exercised the contents envisioned in the previous activity.
FOURTH SESSION Duration: 60 minutes	- A quantitative evaluation (post-test) equivalent to the first (pre-test) was applied.
	- Conducting a focus group.

Fig. 3. Flow of the sessions and their parts

For the analysis, only students who participated in both evaluations (pre and post-test) and attended the face-to-face classroom session were considered ($N = 44$). Table 1 shows the students who performed the pre and post-test along with the corresponding breakdown by gender. The participating teacher was trained for the use of the application for 60 min. Also, to minimize the impact of their skills during the teaching process, a member of the research team was present during the pilot session to ensure that all students received support when faced with difficulties.

2.1 Pedagogical Tools

Two tools were developed for the experiment. The first tool was a set of videos: three classroom videos available to the students after the pre-test and one interactive classroom video used during the classroom-based experimental work.

The videos' format was a formal English lesson delivered by an English teacher on basic English vocabulary. It is worth mentioning that these resources were reviewed and validated by experts in the field in terms of pedagogical content. The group of experts consisted of four professionals: two doctors in education, one doctor with experience in measurement in education and four English teachers (two of them professors of the groups participating in the experiment). Also, two professionals from the multimedia design area were responsible for the production of these resources.

The second pedagogical tool developed was a mobile application (Fig. 4) that allowed students to interact with the Interactive Digital Video classroom. The mobile application was synchronized with the classroom video in seven different moments in the narrative, allowing each student to answer different questions and obtain the corresponding feedback on their devices.

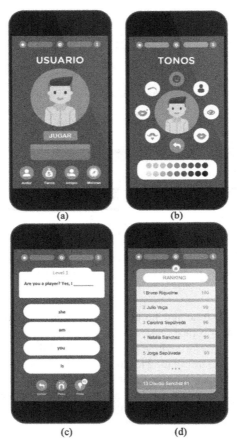

Fig. 4. (a) Main selection module, (b) Avatar configuration interface, (c) Module of questions and alternatives, and (d) Global ranking of student classification.

The application is organized into four modules. The first of them, through a keypad allowing the student to access three other modules: Avatar, Respond and Ranking (see Fig. 4a). In the Avatar module (see Fig. 4b), various elements related to the avatar's appearance associated with the student can be configured, such as the skin color, shape, and color of the eyes, mouth, nose, eyebrows, hair, and beard. In the Respond module (see Fig. 4c), the student can read the question statement, choose one of the five answer alternatives, or use the skip question or request help option. To each correct answer, the student adds 10 points, if it is his first attempt, or otherwise, 5 points. It is worth mentioning that skipping the questions is a limited resource, as well as asking for help, the latter can be, at random, an explanatory text or the elimination of two incorrect alternatives. Finally, in the last module, Ranking (see Fig. 4d), the students can compare their group's top five scores. It should be highlighted that students could continue employing the application after the experiment to practice. Therefore, their positions in the ranking could be affected. It should be remembered that, during the development of this study, students only used the previously described tool to practice English.

2.2 Evaluations

Quantitative Evaluation

The authors developed a quantitative instrument to identify the level of skills in basic English; such an instrument measured the competence of carrying out a personal presentation and delivering tourist information using the verb to be and the grammatical time Simple Present. This instrument was reviewed and validated by group of experts previously mentioned in terms of its pedagogical content and effectiveness in measuring knowledge acquisition.

In paper format, the quantitative assessment instrument contained 33 questions: the first 4 questions asked to describe a sentence in a line; the following 7 questions asked to re-write short sentences of a statement in the negative form; the next 11 asked to fill in blanks, where they should use verbs in Simple Present; in the following 5 questions, the students choose the written correct option between two sentences; and finally, associate 6 words to 6 images. For example, one of the questions to make a self-description was: "Where are you from?". For sentences in negative form, another example was: "John and Mary have two kids". The questions were arranged by level of difficulty (from easy to difficult), to control the effect of position of the item, the operation of the differential item (DIF) and the measurement bias [18]. Cronbach's alpha was used to guarantee the instrument's reliability [19] in each of the participating groups (see Table 2).

Qualitative Evaluation

To determine if the use of Digital Television with multiple screens during a flipped English classroom was related to the level of student of interest in the activity, two moments were analyzed: during the activity with Digital Television and multiple screens and after that. For this, during the experiment, the behavior and the reactions of each participant were recorded, and after the experiment, a group interview was conducted to the students. For the analysis during the experiment, all participants were evaluated individually and classified according to their attitudes, between engaged and dispersed, which was detailed through three broad categories: focused, dispersed and cooperating, and subdivided into behavioral types for a better analysis. This follows the general principles of usability specification table present in the literature [20].

Regarding the group of the semi-structured interviews, these were accompanied by the teacher of each group, to offer support to the students by sharing their experiences and answering the questions of the interviewer [21], a member of the team. The interviews lasted at most 40 min, with a total of five essay questions to give the interviewer more freedom in compiling what the students said. This decision is fundamental not only to collect the positive feedback that may have occurred but also any information that comes to the respondent's mind, be it positive feedback or criticism, as Chaer, Diniz and Ribeiro [22] argue. Some of the guiding questions used were: "What did you think of studying at home only with video lessons and in the classroom doing exercises with the teacher?"; "What do you think about using Interactive Digital Television with a mobile device in the classroom?".

3 Results

3.1 Quantitative

Table 2 shows the average and standard deviations of the pre and post-test scores for each class and the Cronbach Alpha [19] associated with the pre-test. The Shapiro-Wilk test confirmed the assumption of the normality of the pre-test [23]. As seen in Table 2, the post-test score was higher than the pre-test score for each group, although there is a small difference, as could be expected considering the pre-test, in the group of Brazilian students, who in some cases reached the maximum score. The above is consistent with effect size (Cohen's d).

Table 2. Characteristics and scores of each class in the pre-test and post-test

Class	N	Pre-test		Post-test		Cronbach's Alpha	Cohen's d
		M	SD	M	SD		
Brazil	17	29.38	3.52	30.56	2.30	0.837	0.41 (medium effect)
Chile	27	18.89	5.36	20.83	5.44	0.825	0.36 (small effect)

However, to statistically validate the learning process, first the possible difference of previous knowledge (pre-test) between the two groups (classes) must be validated. Levene's test [24] for equality of variances was applied to verify this assumption, which did not reveal significant differences between groups [$F(2, 42) = 2.837, p > .100$]. However, the t-test [25] for equality of means revealed a significant difference [$t(42) = 7.128, p < .00$]. The data allows inferring that each group had different levels of knowledge; however, equally distributed. It should be mentioned that it was not the objective of this study to compare differences between groups, though, the different prior knowledge of the groups allows the development of more meaningful analysis since it shows the possibility of using said technology in different contexts of teaching-learning. To validate that in each group, there were significant learning improvements, an analysis of variance (ANOVA) [26] was carried out, using the pre and post-test instruments' results. The results showed that in both groups there were significant differences between the pre and post-test scores [Brazil $F(1, 16) = -1.67, p < .057$; Chile $F(1, 26) = -2.06, p < .024$]. It is worth mentioning that all statistical analyzes were performed using SPSS, version 24.0.

3.2 Qualitative

Observation

Since the students learned with the use of Digital Television with multiple screens during a flipped classroom, the behavior during that process was studied. For such, the recorded information was analyzed in a range of 10 in 10 s of the video; that interval of time was the longest that allowed discriminating behavior changes. It was observed that the different behaviors (focused, dispersed and cooperating) were grouped in two important events of the activity. The first moment, passive viewer, was characterized by the period where the students watched the video classroom; and the second moment, active viewer, when the student interacted with the classroom video through their mobile device (second screen). Seven moments of active viewer and eight of passive viewer indicated in the figures to be followed were determined.

Figure 5 and 6 show (axis Y) the percentage of the number of categorized behaviors that occurred every 10-s interval (axis X). It can be observed that the levels of concentration, dispersion and cooperation, show that in the moments of Digital Television (DTV), concentration predominates throughout the process, being interrupted by dispersion in most cases. For example, in Chile students were predominantly focused, with a few dispersal behaviors until the first 80 s, when the first moment of interaction with the video begins, which is followed by a predominant behavior change to cooperate. On the other hand, the Brazilian group spent the first 80 s fully focused (see Fig. 6) and then switched to the state mostly cooperating for 20 s until focused with high levels of disruption in the next 20 s.

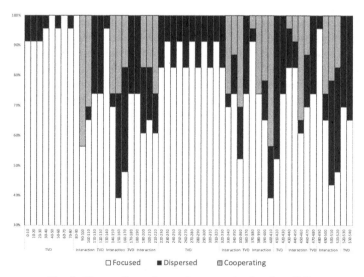

Fig. 5. Focus, dispersion and cooperation levels – Chile

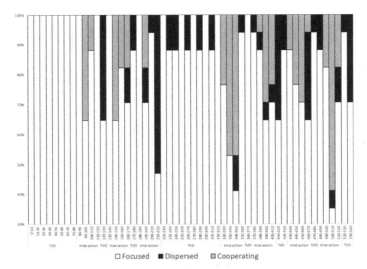

Fig. 6. Focus, dispersion and cooperation levels – Brazil

In summary, the most focused activity can be described during the video on Digital Television (TVD), followed by a transition process from concerted to co-operative or direct during the interaction with Digital Television through the mobile device (Interaction). This transition process can be explained considering the average time needed to answer the questions at each time of interaction. It was observed that as the students answered their questions, the time remaining until resumption of the video classroom, many began to present behaviors of dispersion and/or cooperation. However, it is also possible to highlight, the last 20 s of Chile and 10 s of Brazil, disperse time, for the occasion of the video term, noting that the students with the advance of time in the activity and the increasing complexity of the exercises, they are decreasing their interest.

In summary, Fig. 5 and 6 show that students' engagement during classroom activities was positive. It was possible to verify the predominance of the level of concentration of both Brazilian and Chilean students. In Brazil, 84.2% of students were concentrated, and in Chile, 75.8% were concentrated. Dispersed students accounted for 15.0% in Chile and 7.0% in Brazil. The level of cooperation of Chileans was 9.2% and in Brazilians was 8.8%.

For a more detailed analysis of participants' behaviors during the activity, the focused, dispersed and cooperating categories were subdivided. The first, focused, was divided into: serious, laughing and talking with a classmate (see Fig. 7 and 8, Chile and Brazil respectively). It should be mentioned that serious concentration predominates (Chile: 88.8% and Brazil: 87.4%). Focused laughter was 3.1% in Chile and 2.1% in Brazil. Finally, 10.5% of Brazilians and 8.1% of Chileans participated in a focused conversation with a classmate. It is worth highlighting the difference in the classroom environment between the two countries. In Chile, daily, students are distributed in pairs, which in some way strengthens the collaboration among students, but during this work, this position was not granted; they were distributed individually, this is the most common classroom distribution in Brazil. This fact may explain this result.

Analyzing the predominant types of concentration in Chile and Brazil, we can observe the full dominance of the serious focused behavior throughout the process.

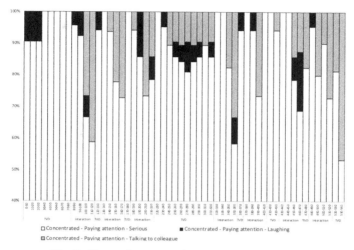

Fig. 7. Types of concentration - students from Chile

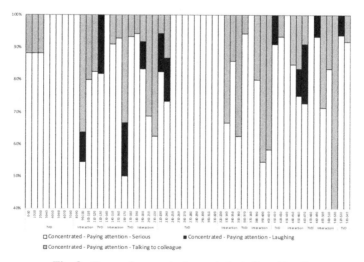

Fig. 8. Types of concentration - students from Brazil

The second category, dispersed, was subdivided into dispersed - talking with a classmate and dispersed - alone. The dispersion was less prevalent, but it occurred and can be observed in Fig. 9 (Chile) and Fig. 10 (Brazil). In Chile, the dispersion was 61% alone and 39% talking with a classmate, that is, there was a predominance of dispersion alone, but in the final part of the activity, it became a dispersion talking with a classmate.

In Brazil, the total predominance was the type talking with a classmate (70%), while 30% of the students were dispersed alone.

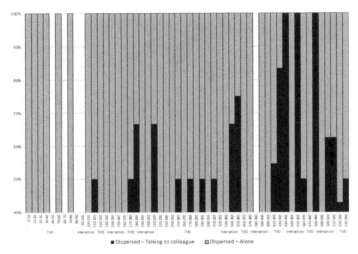

Fig. 9. Types of dispersion - students from Chile

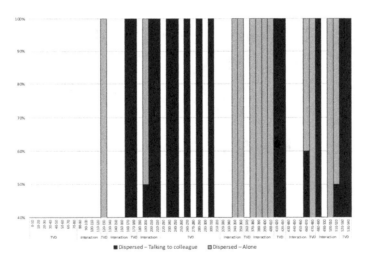

Fig. 10. Types of dispersion - students from Brazil

The third category, cooperating, consisting of the types helping the friend to respond and observing the responding friend, analyzed graphically from Fig. 11 and 12, Chile and Brazil, respectively, indicate the interaction of the students during the activity and its totality represents 8.8% in Chile and 9.2% in Brazil. The predominant result in both countries is that students cooperate more by observing than by helping their classmates (in Chile, 90.4% of the students observed the classmate respond, in Brazil, 96.3%). Something to consider is that in the case of Chile this help for the classmates occurred in the second moment of interaction with the application, an action that in Brazil is focused only on the end of the activity. Regarding interaction, this can be observed always occurring. However, it is worth mentioning that in Chile and Brazil, student interaction occurs after the first 10 s, in five of the seven moments of interaction with the video lesson. In the fourth interaction, Chilean students continue interacting after the 10 s, while Brazilian students interacted from the beginning; Chileans interacted until the end and Brazilians do not interact in the last 10 s. In the fifth moment, Chilean students interact throughout the process, while Brazilian ones begin interacting after 10 s. Already in the sixth moment, the two groups interact integrally. In the seventh and last interaction, both Chilean and Brazilian students interact from the 10th second and go on to the end.

Regarding the fact that the interaction starts at five moments, after the 10 s, in the two groups, it can be suggested that the students, when assimilating the video, used this time to speculate the answers. Another observed fact is that Chilean students maintained a greater regularity throughout the process, while ones from Brazil, in the initial moments, presented a certain irregularity in the interaction, as in the third moment, in which the students interacted in only 10 s out of a total of 40 s, which characterizes ease in resolving the exercise at that time. However, in the final moments, students from Chile and Brazil displayed a focused behavior on interaction, which may mean the need for collaboration to solve problems, given the higher degree of difficulty.

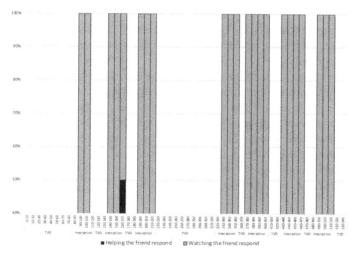

Fig. 11. Types of cooperation - students from Chile

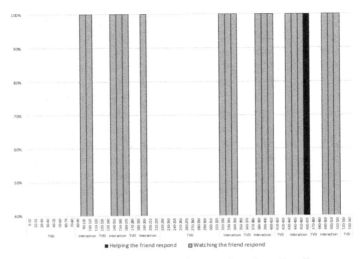

Fig. 12. Types of cooperation - students from Brazil

Interviews

At the end of the multi-screen experience, a group interview was conducted (open interviews). As a result, students' enthusiasm and curiosity about the applied technology can be highlighted, despite an apparent shyness in replying to the investigator's questions. Also, it was possible to observe a predominance of brief answers, not deepened, and the desire for more activities like this in the classroom. About the experience as a whole, the Chilean students considered it "interesting", "flashy", "fun" and "different, but fun", including one of the students pointed out that this method provides greater ease in learning the contents.

Similarly, Brazilian students have described the use of Digital Television with multiple screens as making learning "lighter", "cool", "dynamics", "different and interesting, but it cannot be just that way". In this sense, a student mentioned the supposed need to intercalate the classes with the Digital Television and the normal ones (traditional), but that it would require an adaptation process. An advantage pointed out in one of the comments mentions the possibility that this method would allow the teacher to evaluate the students' performance daily, "being evaluated every day is better than waiting for the result of a test to know where your difficulties lie."

4   Discussion and Future Work

The impact of the use of Digital Television with multiple screens during a flipped English classroom was analyzed for 59 third-year high school students in Brazil and Chile. The participants studied for two consecutive weeks, using the flipped class method with multiple screens. The results showed that all the groups have improved their knowledge of English.

Another observed result was the high degree of student appreciation concerning the use of Digital Television with multiple screens during a flipped English class, a fact that can be explained by the expectations of today's young people regarding technology, as well as by the strength of the audiovisual and its innovations in the daily lives of this generation. Although flipped learning is not restricted to the use of videos, it was noticed the great influence of these contents on the participants, especially when interacting with the mobile application, which enabled students to exercise autonomy and learn in an active and playful way. Despite the cultural differences, the collaboration and cooperation seen in both countries revealed a common desire among students to have more opportunities to learn using Digital TV and multiple screens. It should be noted that the importance of this study lies in showing that when multiple screens are used, the student is affected by technology not only in the efficiency of their learning but also because it opens opportunities to break down structures rooted in the teaching profession.

Finally, the limitations are part of any research in the classroom and, thus, should be considered. The first limitation of this study comes from the sample's size and representativeness since only two technical high schools and only a portion of the available levels were analyzed; a representative sample (including non-technical schools) would have allowed the generalization and analysis for gender of the results. The second limitation is associated with the reduced number of sessions; a larger number of sessions would have allowed analyzing how the contributions of the application's use in the quality of knowledge and observing student interest over time. Lastly, interview method should be reshaped to evaluate with more precision how flipped classroom influence this kind of scenario, checking more accurately whether behaviors identified were also influenced by the typology of content or learning activity; also, considering the students' background regarding their use of technology and their previous motivations to use it in the classroom, so this information can be compared with the data from the experience itself, gathered during the sessions.

Acknowledgements. This work was supported by the Comisión Nacional de Investigación Científica y Tecnológica (CONICYT) [grant number REDI170043] and Dirección de Investigación, Postgrado y Transferencia Tecnológica at Universidad de Tarapacá.

References

1. Diesel, A., Santos Baldez, A.L., Neumann Martins, S.: Os princípios das metodologias ativas de ensino: uma abordagem teórica. Revista Thema **14**(1), 268–288 (2017)
2. Selwyn, N.: Educação e Tecnologia: questões críticas. In: Ferreira, G.M.S., Rosado, L.A.S., Carvalho, J. S. (eds.) Educação e Tecnologia: abordagens críticas. 1st edn. pp. 85–104. SESES, Rio de Janeiro (2017)
3. Sampaio, M.N., Leite, L.S.: Alfabetização tecnológica do professor, 7th edn. Vozes, Petrópolis, RJ, BR (2010)
4. Morán, J.: Mudando a educação com metodologias ativas. Coleção Mídias Contemporâneas. Convergências Midiáticas, Educação e Cidadania: aproximações jovens **2**(1), 15–33 (2015).
5. Berbel, N.A.N.: As metodologias ativas e a promoção da autonomia dos estudantes. Semina: Ciências Sociais e Humanas **32**(1), 25–40 (2011)
6. Beserra, V., Angeluci, A.C.B., Pedroso, R.G., Navarrete, M.: A systematic literature review of iDTV in learning contexts. In: Abásolo, M., Silva, T., González, N. (eds.) Iberoamerican Conference on Applications and Usability of Interactive TV, pp. 3–13. Springer, Cham (2018). https://doi.org/10.1007/978-3-030-23862-9_1

7. Barbosa, E.F., de Moura, D.G.: Metodologias ativas de aprendizagem na Educação Profissional e Tecnológica. Boletim Técnico Do Senac **39**(2), 48–67 (2013)
8. Bacich, L., Neto, A.T., de Mello Trevisani, F.: Ensino híbrido: personalização e tecnologia na educação. Penso Editora, Porto Alegre, BR (2015)
9. Bergmann, J., Sams, A.: Sala de aula invertida: uma metodologia ativa de aprendizagem, 1st edn. LTC, Rio de Janeiro (2018)
10. Bergmann, J.: Solving the homework problem by flipping the learning. ASCD, Alexandria, VA, USA (2019)
11. Suhr, I.R.F.: Implantação de cursos semipresenciais usando a metodologia da sala de aula invertida: limites e possibilidades a partir do olhar dos professores envolvidos. In: Congresso Nacional de Educação, EDUCERE, vol. 12, pp. 32714–32726. PUC-PR, Curitiba (2015)
12. Divardin, D.C.: O audiovisual na educação brasileira: do cinema educativo às tecnologias digitais. In: Congresso Brasileiro de Ciências da Comunicação, INTERCOM, vol 38. Intercom, Rio de Janeiro (2015)
13. Prata, A., Chambel, T.: Mobility in crossmedia systems, the design challenges that need to be addressed. In: 8th Iberoamerican Conference on Applications and Usability of Interactive TV, pp. 67–86. Springer, Cham (2019). https://doi.org/10.1007/978-3-030-56574-9_5
14. Talbert, R.: Inverted classroom. Colleagues **9**(1), 1–3 (2012)
15. De Grande, F.C., Américo, M.: A TV digital e as plataformas multidigitais no Chile. Revista Extraprensa **11**(1), 24–38 (2017)
16. Silva, T., Almeida, P., Cardoso, B., Oliveira, R., Cunha, A., Ribeiro, C.: Smartly: a TV companion app to deliver discount coupons. In: 8th Iberoamerican Conference on Applications and Usability of Interactive TV, pp. 53–66. Springer, Cham (2019). https://doi.org/10.1007/978-3-030-56574-9_4
17. Beserra, V., Quaglio, A.M., Falandes, C.G.: Reflexões sobre o ensino híbrido: uso da sala de aula invertida em cenários inovadores com TV digital e múltiplas telas. Educação & Linguagem **21**(1), 5–22 (2018)
18. Thissen, D., Steinberg, L., Wainer, H.: Detection of differential item functioning using the parameters of item response models. In: Holland, P.W., Wainer, H. (eds.) Differential Item Functioning, pp. 67–113. Lawrence Erlbaum Associates Inc., Hillsdale, NJ, US (1993)
19. Tavakol, M., Dennick, R.: Making sense of cronbach's alpha. Int. J. Med. Educ. **2**, 53–55 (2011)
20. Hix, D., Hartson, H.R.: Developing User Interfaces: Ensuring Usability Through Product and Process. Wiley, New York (1997)
21. Nel, N.M., Romm, N.R.A., Tlale, L.D.N.: Reflections on focus group sessions regarding inclusive education: reconsidering focus group research possibilities. Aust. Educ. Res. **42**(1), 35–53 (2014). https://doi.org/10.1007/s13384-014-0150-3
22. Chaer, G., Diniz, R.R.P., Ribeiro, E.A.: A técnica do questionário na pesquisa educacional. Revista Evidência **7**(7), 251–266 (2012)
23. Curran-Everett, D.: Explorations in statistics: the assumption of normality. Adv. Physiol. Educ. **41**(3), 449–453 (2017)
24. Nordstokke, D.W., Zumbo, B.D.: A new nonparametric Levene test for equal variances. Psicológica **31**(2), 401–430 (2010)
25. Gerald, B.: A brief review of independent, dependent and one sample t-test. Int. J. Appl. Math. Theoret. Phys. **4**(2), 50–54 (2018)
26. Keselman, H.J., et al.: Statistical practices of educational researchers: an analysis of their ANOVA, MANOVA, and ANCOVA analyses. Rev. Educ. Res. **68**(3), 350–386 (1998)

From the Living Room to the Classroom and Back – Production Guidelines for Science Videos

Carolina Almeida(⊠) 📵 and Pedro Almeida📵

University of Aveiro – Digimedia, Aveiro, Portugal
{carol,almeida}@ua.pt

Abstract. After finding the audiovisual preferences of teenagers about online videos and following a design-based research planning, a set of videos about natural sciences concepts was produced. These videos were published on YouTube following a communication strategy with posts on social networks (Facebook, Instagram and Twitter) in a 13 days period. On a group session, 8 teenagers evaluated original videos and the related communication strategy. On the same session teenagers were asked about the possibility of watching similar videos in future occasions.

A total of 6 teachers were also consulted in order to validate their willingness to recommend educational videos similar to the prototyped ones to their students.

The videos were appreciated and almost all the features were validated by the teenagers. Teachers revealed open to recommend such videos.

The results from the teenagers and teachers' evaluations resulted in a set of guidelines for the production and sharing of educational videos that may be useful for teachers and other educational players.

Keywords: Online video · Production guidelines · Educational video

1 Introduction

Teenagers, aged between 12 and 16 years old in 2016, were classified as part of Generation Z. This Generation is defined, among other dimensions, by its behaviors towards media usage [1]. They are heavy consumers of video, mainly on mobile devices [2], and have been shifting their watching routines from linear TV to streaming platforms [3]. According to Deloitte, the youngest of this age group are the people born in 1997 [4]. The described behaviors and definition of Generation Z was identified on the US population but Portuguese teenagers also follow the trend [5]. Time spent watching streaming contents and the percentage of mobile data used for it were increasing since 2010 for this age group [3].

© Springer Nature Switzerland AG 2021
M. J. Abásolo et al. (Eds.): jAUTI 2020, CCIS 1433, pp. 77–88, 2021.
https://doi.org/10.1007/978-3-030-81996-5_6

This project was carried on the potential of taking advantage of some of the time spent watching entertainment videos to promote informal learning through education videos. Based on the conclusions of previous studies about teenagers' preferences towards online video, a set of prototyped videos were produced. Production tasks are explained on Sect. 3, more precisely on Subsect. 3.2.

The main goal of this research was to evaluate the dimensions of the videos (host, editing pace, scenario, soundtrack, length, animation, infographics, speech pace, speech style, language and content density), briefly described on Table 1, and check if they correspond to the previously identified preferences [6], counting on the feedback from a sample of users (teenagers aged 12–16). It was also a goal to identify how the teenagers usually choose the videos to watch and evaluate their willingness to include similar videos in their entertainment routines.

Based on the conclusions, a set of guidelines useful to anyone interested in producing similar educational videos would be the final desired output.

In the next section, Sect. 2, some production guidelines that apply to formal and informal learning videos and also popular YouTube videos are reviewed.

2 State of the Art

A review on previously available guidelines was relevant to develop the proposed prototyped videos. In this section previously available guidelines on production of formal learning videos, science communication videos, informal learning videos and also the popular YouTube videos are presented. This review allowed us to find the common aspects upon different kinds of educational videos.

Formal learning videos have been analyzed by several authors [7, 8]. These studies have identified some principles such as optioning for shorter lengths or the use of graphical elements (animations, graphs or even manuscript notes) for concepts demonstrations [9]. Videos with such features were correlated with better results in what concerns knowledge construction and students' organization of their learning [9]. Signaling the most relevant ideas and limiting the number of concepts per video was correlated to a decrease of the students' perception of difficulty of the concepts on the video [10].

Regarding science communication videos they are already available on YouTube being produced by researchers, research teams or even public or private institutions. The most popular ones are short length (2–3 min), comic, with animations and sound effects [11].

Informal educational channels such Kurzgesagt – In a Nutshell[1], Crash course[2], or Vsauce[3], followed by more than 16 million users (as in February 2021), share the use of animations (Fig. 1, left) and a relaxed style of speech. The last two included an onscreen host (Fig. 1, right).

---

[1] Kurzgesagt – In a Nutshell: https://bit.ly/1h4rc74.

[2] Crash Course: https://www.youtube.com/user/crashcourse.

[3] Vsauce: https://bit.ly/1cGr5uI.

Fig. 1. Animation on Kurzgesagt (left) and relaxed style host on Crash Course videos (right).

Among the most popular YouTube channels it is possible to identify shared characteristics in its videos such as fast speech, fast editing pace with wider use of jump cuts [12] and also comic appointments (e.g. inside jokes) [12, 13].

Having in mind the presented contributions to understand the dimensions behind the online video popularity or their effectiveness to promote learning on different contexts, the methods followed to extend the contributions to the field are presented on the next section.

3 Methods

In order to develop a set of guidelines for the production and sharing of educational videos two cycles of development, publication and evaluation were planned according to Design Based Research [14], a methodology plan in which conclusions of each cycle affect the development of the next cycle and counts on users impressions to develop a product or intervention. On Sect. 3.1 the sample of participants is described, on Sect. 3.2 the main stages of the study are described and, on Sect. 3.3, the way data was processed is explained.

3.1 Participants

The study gathers the impressions of two groups of teenagers, 4 on the pre-test and 8 on the final evaluation. All of them were aged between 12 and 16 years old and attended public schools on Portugal (7th to 9th grade).

The last phase comprised two groups of teachers, a group of 3 young teachers with less than a year of work experience and a group of 3 experienced teachers counting more than ten years of teaching practice.

3.2 Stages Description

Based on the conclusions of a previous evaluation phase carried by the researchers [6] the study was distributed in two additional phases as illustrated on Fig. 2.

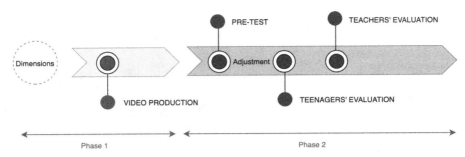

Fig. 2. Phases of the study

On that referred preliminary evaluation phase (described in detail on a previous publication [6]), teenagers approved the following dimensions (see Table 1) as appreciated ones in online videos. These include technical, speech and content density characteristics.

Table 1. Description of the dimensions appreciated by the participants on the evaluation stage.

Technical	
Onscreen host	Participant and onscreen host
Fast paced editing	Wide use of jump cuts
Virtual scenario	Host capture on chromakey to allow the introduction of virtual scenarios
Sound effects	Animations and props highlighted with sound effects
Background music	Introduction of background music along the video
Length	Short length, between 2 to 3 min
2D animation	Animated draws (without the idea of space)
Speech	
Plain language	Concepts explained without technical jargon
Relaxed style	Host uses colloquial style with some comic references
Fast paced speech	Host speaks fast
Content density	
Light approach	Contents are briefly presented without many details

The first of the two additional phases consisted on the production, postproduction and construction of the communication strategy. The following phase consisted on the dissemination and evaluation of the prototyped videos and its communication strategy. The first phase was implemented from November 2016 to October 2017. The second phase started on November 2017 and finished on May 2018.

First Phase – Video Production

The first phase of this study included the pre-production tasks (script writing) the host casting, image and sound capture activities and the postproduction tasks. The personalization of the YouTube channel and the social networks pages and profiles (banner and profile picture) was also developed (see Fig. 3). The schedule of posts (Facebook mainly and Instagram) and the video publication was the last activity included in this phase.

Fig. 3. Preview of the YouTube channel "Coisa Ciência" (February 18th 2021).

A total of three videos about natural sciences themes were produced, namely about plate tectonics, vulcanism and seismicity. The list of concepts addressed in each video is described in the next page, on Fig. 4.

Second Phase – Teenagers' Evaluation

On November 2017 the original videos were released, according to the schedule developed on the previous phase. On a work 4 teenagers gave their evaluation about the videos and the communication strategy.

Following the conclusions of the pre-test, the videos weren't modified but a new communication strategy was developed, including the preparation of posts on Twitter, Instagram and also on Facebook.

Videos were republished on January 2018 and evaluated on another work session, described above, on Fig. 5, with 8 teenagers on February 2018 on a living room.

Second Phase – Teachers' Evaluation

According to the students' inputs on the previous two stages a final evaluation on the original videos was planned. Sessions included watching the video, answer to a questionnaire and an interview. The sessions were booked with each teacher on May 2018. All the sessions were planned according to the order showed on Fig. 6. The interview was in-person for the experienced teachers and for one of the young teachers. The other two young teachers were interviewed on a videoconference call.

TITLE / THUMBNAIL	CONCEPTS
#1 Moving plates. **#1 PLACAS EM MOVIMENTO**	Convection currents Physical internal model of Earth Divergent boundary Convergent boundary
#2 There's a volcano under your house. **#2 TENS UM VULCÃO DEBAIXO DE TUA CASA!**	Divergent boundary Convergent boundary Transformative boundary Seismicity Volcanism
#3 Where did the mountains go? **#3 PARA ONDE FORAM AS MONTANHAS?**	Convergent boundary Orogenic movements – mountain formation

Fig. 4. List of concepts addressed in each original video

Stage 1	Stage 2	Stage 3

Watch the original videos on a TV set	Answer to a printed questionnaire	Participate on a Focus Group

Fig. 5. Planning of the work sessions with teenagers.

Stage 1	Stage 2	Stage 3

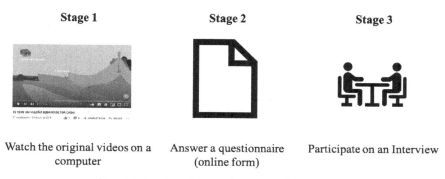

Watch the original videos on a computer	Answer a questionnaire (online form)	Participate on an Interview

Fig. 6. Planning of the work session with teachers.

3.3 Data Processing

Answers to the questionnaires, both from teenagers and teachers, were subjected to descriptive statistics analysis. Focus group discussions and the interviews were transcribed and analyzed on its content. Data from the interviews and focus group was used to complement the main data source, the answers to the questionnaire.

4 Results

Prototyped videos featured onscreen host, virtual scenario and animations. These dimensions are illustrated on Fig. 7. The videos were fast paced edited, included all the same background music and sound effects. The host speech was fast paced and used a limited number of technical words to approach in low detail the phenomena or concepts presented. The style of speech was relaxed with humoristic appointments.

Fig. 7. Onscreen host on virtual scenario (left), 2D animations (center) and infographics (right) examples from prototyped videos.

4.1 Students' Evaluation

According to the answers to the questionnaire, presented below on Fig. 8, it was possible to validate almost all the features of the original videos as appreciated features matching the teenagers' preferences. The exceptions to a unanimous approval were the use of background music, sound effects and infographics, but still with positive approval. Nevertheless, some isolated unappreciation about some particular frames was expressed during the focus group. For example, although fast paced speech was a clear preference, at some points of the videos it was perceived to be an obstacle to the correct understanding of the concepts being presented. Similar impressions were shared about the level of detail of explanations: a light or general approach to concepts is pleasant but some participants (2 in 8) agreed that a deeper approach would be welcomed to explain some of the concepts on one of the videos.

Features Unapreciated	Dimension Subdimension and Category	Features Apreciated
	Technical	
| | | | | | | |	Onscreen host	| | | | | | | |
| | | | | | | |	Fast paced edition	| | | | | | | |
| | | | | | | |	Virtual scenario	| | | | | | | |
| | | | | | | | |	Sound effects	| | | | | | | |
| | | | | | | | |	Backgroud music	| | | | | | | | |
| | | | | | | |	Lenght (2-3 min)	| | | | | | | |
| | | | | | | |	2D animation	| | | | | | | |
| | | | | | | | |	Infographics	| | | | | | | |
	Speech	
| | | | | | | |	Plain language	| | | | | | | |
| | | | | | | | |	Relaxed style (with humour)	| | | | | | | |
| | | | | | | |	Fast paced speech	| | | | | | | |
	Content Density	
| | | | | | | |	Light Approach	| | | | | | | |

Fig. 8. Results from teenagers' evaluation, collected from their answers to the questionnaire (N = 8).

Previous to the session, 6 in 8 participants had already interacted with the YouTube channel were the videos were published. Thematic indexation of videos was a valued feature for 5 in 8 participants. They valued it since they are used to choose the contents to watch on their subscriptions' page.

In overall, they enjoyed watching the videos (5 in 8) but weren't available to watch it during their leisure times (5 in 8). But they all demonstrated to be interested in watching similar videos on classroom or during study sessions. More details on the subject are available on previous publications [6, 15].

4.2 Teachers' Evaluation

Teachers, consulted after the students had expressed their willingness to watch proto-typed videos as study or classroom resources, agreed with the possibility of recommending similar videos in their classes. The teachers' results, collected from the answers to the questionnaire and to the interviews, are condensed on Fig. 9.

Features Unappreciated		Dimension Subdimension and Category	Features Appreciated	
		Technical		
I I I	I I I	Present host	I I I	I I I
I I I	I I I	Fast paced edition	I I I	I I I
I I I	I I I	Virtual scenario	I I I	I I I
I I I	I I I	Sound effects	I I I	I I I
I I I	I I I	Backgroud music	I I I	I I I
I I I	I I I	Lenght (2-3 min)	I I I	I I I
I I I	I I I	2D animation	I I I	I I I
I I I	I I I	Infographics	I I I	I I I
		Speech		
I I I	I I I	Plain language	I I I	I I I
I I I	I I I	Relaxed style (with humour)	I I I	I I I
I I I	I I I	Fast paced speech	I I I	I I I
		Content Density		
I I I	I I I	Light Approach	I I I	I I I

Fig. 9. Results from teachers' evaluation, collected from their answers to the questionnaire and interview (young teachers N = 3; experienced teachers N = 3).

Teachers validated many features of the videos. Infographics were a unanimous validated feature for both groups of teachers (3 in 3 for the young teachers; 3 in 3 for the experienced teachers). The simple approach to content presentation was validated by all the young teachers (3 in 3). The sequence of ideas, not mentioned on Fig. 9, was appreciated by all the experienced teachers (3 in 3).

With a negative validation fast paced speech and editing stands out. Combining the answers to the questionnaire with the answers to the interview, fast paced speech was unappreciated by all teachers (3 young and 3 experienced) and the almost the same validation was found for fast paced editing. Only one young teacher didn't mention the fast-paced feature as an obstacle to the concepts' understanding.

2D animation was unappreciated by the experienced teachers (2 in 3 experienced teachers).

In order to increase fidelity on natural phenomena representation the experienced teachers suggested some improvements, such as considering the use of 3D animations. They also suggested the segmentation of the prototyped videos in order to address less topics per video with the same length. This way, and with a slower paced speech, the videos would improve their usability as educational resources. One of the experienced teachers suggested also to develop, besides the small segments of video, longer clips to be used as a synthesis educational resource. In order to complement the missing information of the simple approach to the concepts, one of the experienced teachers also suggested adding hyperlinks to the videos.

Having in mind the different didactic uses of videos similar to the prototyped ones, all young teachers were willing to use such videos to be watched pre-class (e.g. in flipped classroom approaches), as a discussion starter, as a summary or as study material (last three uses recommended by 2 in 3).

Experienced teachers were also open to different didactic uses of videos similar to the prototyped ones. They were open to recommend such videos as summaries (3 in 3), as a pre-class resource (1 in 3) or even as informative resources to introduce concepts in class (1 in 3).

5   Conclusions

Following the results of this exploratory study, some production recommendations can be highlighted and be useful to teachers and other content creators. Since students are open to the pedagogical integration of such videos the production of such content gains more relevance.

Following the features identified on popular videos, and later validated in the following evaluations by the researchers we may conclude that the following dimensions are appreciated by teenagers in educational videos:

- The use of an onscreen host;
- A relaxed style of speech;
- A fast paced speech;
- The use of simple and plain language;
- Short length videos;

- The integration of different kinds of animations;
- The use of virtual scenarios;
- The use of fast-paced editing;
- The integration of music or sound effects.

The enounced dimensions are appreciated by teenagers and should figure in educational videos. But content creators can also take in consideration additional conclusions from this study. The length of the videos should be proportional to the number of concepts addressed and the level of detail in explanations. Although virtual scenarios are valued by teenagers, using different kinds of scenarios can also be recommended. Although teenagers prefer a faster paced editing and speech, slower pace can be recommended when the purpose is to the deliver contents for formal learning contexts. When choosing the animation style to represent a natural phenomenon, 3D animations should be considered, especially if there is the need to represent deepness, for example, when representing a conservative plate boundary when the plates move laterally only.

All the referred principles apply to natural sciences videos but can be applied to videos about other subjects.

Considering that the interactions with the videos occurred mainly on YouTube, careful thematic indexation is advised in order to ease the searching tasks, for example when the students need to review concepts and find a video for that.

This research was developed before the 2020 pandemic crisis that obliged governments to close schools and forced all the educational communities to shift to distance learning scenarios. The listed guidelines, which were already useful before the pandemic situation can be even more valid during challenging times where e-learning and b-learning practices are increasingly important, and teachers face the need to deliver contents remotely.

References

1. Dimock, M.: Defining generations: Where millennials end and generation Z begins (2019)
2. Ericsson ConsumerLab: Tv and Media 2015 (2015)
3. Deloitte Development: Digital media trends survey (2018)
4. Edelman, K., Hurley, B., Nairita, G.: Digital media trends survey, 14th edn. (2020)
5. Velhinho, A., Fernandes, S., Abreu, J., Almeida, P., Silva, T.: Field trial of a new iTV approach: the potential of Its UX among younger audiences. In: Abásolo, M.J., Silva, T., González, N.D. (eds.) jAUTI 2018. CCIS, vol. 1004, pp. 131–147. Springer, Cham (2019). https://doi.org/10.1007/978-3-030-23862-9_10
6. Almeida, C., Almeida, P.: Online educational videos: the teenagers' preferences. In: Almeida, P., Amargós, J., Abásolo, M.J. (eds.) Applications and Usability of Interactive TV, pp. 65–76. Springer, La Habana (2017)
7. Chen, C.-M., Wu, C.-H.: Effects of different video lecture types on sustained attention, emotion, cognitive load, and learning performance. Comput. Educ. **80**, 108–121 (2015). https://doi.org/10.1016/j.compedu.2014.08.015
8. Chorianopoulos, K., Giannakos, M.N.: Usability design for video lectures. In: Proceedings of the 11th European Conference on Interactive TV Video - EuroITV 2013, 163–164 (2013). https://doi.org/10.1145/2465958.2465982

9. Ou, C., Goel, A.K., Joyner, D.A., Haynes, D.F.: Designing videos with pedagogical strategies : online students' perceptions of their effectiveness. In: Proceedings of 3rd ACM Conference Learning Scale Conferencec - L@S 2016, pp. 141–144 (2016). https://doi.org/10.1145/287 6034.2893391

10. Douglas, S.S., Aiken, J.M., Greco, E., Schatz, M., Lin, S.-Y.: Do-it-yourself whiteboard-style physics video lectures. Phys. Teach. **55**, 22–24 (2017). https://doi.org/10.1119/1.4972492

11. Schneider, F.M., Weinmann, C., Roth, F.S., Knop, K., Vorderer, P.: Learning from entertaining online video clips? Enjoyment and appreciation and their differential relationships with knowledge and behavioral intentions. Comput. Human Behav. **54**, 475–482 (2016). https://doi.org/10.1016/j.chb.2015.08.028

12. Cunningham, S., Craig, D.: Being 'really real' on YouTube: authenticity, community and brand culture in social media entertainment. Media Int. Aust. **164**, 71–81 (2017). https://doi.org/10.1177/1329878X17709098

13. Himma-Kadakas, M.: The food chain of YouTubers: engaging audiences with formats and genres. Observatory 54–75 (2018). https://doi.org/10.15847/obsOBS0001385

14. Van den Akker, J.: Principles and methods of development research. In: Van den Akker, J., Branch, R.M., Gustafson, K., Nieveen, N., Plomp, T. (eds.) Design Approaches and Tools in Education and Training, pp. 1–14. Springer, Dordrecht (1999). https://doi.org/10.1007/978-94-011-4255-7_1

15. Almeida, C., Almeida, P.: Online educational videos : how to produce them according to teenagers' preferences and teachers' approval. In: Proceedings of jAuti20 - IX Iberoamerican Conference on Applications and Usability for Interactive TV, Aveiro, Portugal, 18 December 2020 (2020)

Personalized Interactive Video-Based Crosmedia Informal Learning Environments from iTV, PC and Mobile Devices – The Design Challenges

Alcina Prata[1](✉) [iD] and Teresa Chambel[2](✉) [iD]

[1] Superior School of Business Management (ESCE),
Polytechnic Institute of Setúbal, Setúbal, Portugal
Alcina.prata@esce.ips.pt
[2] Lasige, Faculty of Sciences, University of Lisbon, Lisbon, Portugal
mtchambel@ciencias.ulisboa.pt

Abstract. Television always had an important role in everyday life. However, due to several circumstances, as the proliferation of new devices with improved technological characteristics, better interfaces and better communication features, the TV viewing/use paradigm evolved to a new level. Television is now often used as part of crossmedia systems, thus creating flexible solutions so helpful when learning environments and different contexts of use are the main goal. This paper briefly addresses the design challenges that need to be considered in the design of crossmedia systems able to generate personalized video-based interactive informal learning environments from iTV, PC and mobile devices. The system that was designed to illustrate our research, and which evolved from previous versions, is called eiTV (meaning interactive TV content extended and complemented with web contents) and generates a crossmedia personalized informal video-based learning environment, through the form of a web-based content, which provides extra information about users' selected topics of interest while watching a specific video. The web content may be generated, accessed and personalized through iTV, PC and mobile devices and, depending on the users' needs, viewed immediately or stored for latter view, individually or simultaneously, also from iTV, PC and mobile devices.

An evaluation, with the participation of 90 elements, from 18 to 65 years old, grouped into 3 different age groups, was carried out with high fidelity prototypes and the achieved results were very optimistic considering that they helped rethink our crossmedia related assumptions and showed that the exploration of new functionalities and solutions was a success amongst the different age groups.

Keywords: Television · Crossmedia · Transmedia · Informal learning · Learning environment

1 Introduction

Our world is an increasingly crossmedia world. In fact, crossmedia and transmedia systems, environments and applications are prospering in practically all areas [1–3].

© Springer Nature Switzerland AG 2021
M. J. Abásolo et al. (Eds.): jAUTI 2020, CCIS 1433, pp. 89–104, 2021.
https://doi.org/10.1007/978-3-030-81996-5_7

Crossmedia systems refers to those where the same message is distributed through different channels/platforms (repetition) while on transmedia systems, the message is expanded through different devices/platforms (expansion) [1, 2]. The success and adoption of crossmedia and transmedia environments is impacted by many factors as for instance the proliferation of new and appealing devices capable to support human activities across different contextual settings, technological advances as faster internet access, viewers changes in terms of technological interests and habits (mainly triggered by the appearance of some killer applications as social networks) and the systems characteristics, which the most relevant are, flexibility and mobility, so essential to support today's lifestyle [3]. One of the areas where crossmedia and transmedia systems has been achieving very good results is the area of informal learning environments and contexts [4–6].

In what relates to the medium used to support learning through crossmedia systems, video is, clearly, one of the richest ones. As to the devices used to access video, TV, PC and, more recently, mobile devices, are the privileged ones depending on the age range. Through structure and interaction, these devices can open the door to flexible environments that can access video and integrate it with different media, accessible from different devices, adequate to support different cognitive modes and learning processes in several contexts. Despite their valuable potential to create rich and flexible environments, the design of these crossmedia environments/systems faces some challenges that may affect their effective use. More important than technical details are crossmedia conceptual aspects such as interaction and service design based on cognitive processes, usability, user experience, contextualization, continuity, media affordances, and device characteristics. Our main concern has been to focus also and mainly on these aspects, while studying and understanding this emerging paradigm, where research has not been complete [7].

Our eiTV system has been designed and developed to illustrate our research and has been through an evolution process of 3 generations of prototypes, all ranging from low to high fidelity prototypes. The third generation prototypes, briefly presented in this paper, were the richer ones in terms of devices and functionalities involved, which increased to match a more flexible perspective. Running from iTV, PC and mobile devices, it provides users with the possibility to choose, from a video, usually watched in a more experiential cognitive mode (which allows us to perceive and react to events naturally), which topics they would want to know more about. They may also choose with which level of detail, and later decide when and where they would want to access those extra related contents (informal learning environments, generated from iTV, PC and mobile devices, presented through the form of a web-based content), in a more reflective mode (the mode of thought), and with whom they would want to share them with, having the adequate support from the application in the different access contexts. Important to refer that, to simplify, the mentioned generated web-based extra related content, also referred to as crossmedia informal learning environment, will be referred along the text, simply, as web content. The architecture and the main features available in iTV, PC and mobile contexts were already explored and described on previous publications [4, 5, 8], but never tested as a whole and completely integrated system by three different age ranges, as presented on this paper.

After this introduction, Sect. 2 includes a review of related work and concepts, Sect. 3 describes the design challenges of crossmedia applications in that context, Sect. 4 presents some of the most important design decisions, Sect. 5 describes the evaluation process and, finally, Sect. 6 presents the conclusions and perspectives for future research and developments.

2 Related Work

This section addresses some of the more relevant related research studies in Crossmedia environments that include the same or similar devices and/or have informal/formal learning goals.

The TAMALLE project [9] developed a 'dual device system' for informal English language learning, based on watching iTV and selecting what to access later on mobile phones. This was an interesting system capable to accommodate different cognitive modes and different contexts of use, especially, if considering the mobile phone possibilities. Obrist et al. [10] developed a "6 key navigation model" and its interface for an electronic program guide running on the TV, PC and mobile phone. The different devices were not used in a complementary way since the intention was to test a similar interface, on three different devices. They have perceived that viewers prefer a reduced number of navigation keys and a unified UI with the same functionalities across devices. This confirmed our prototypes UI design last decisions. Newstream [11] provides extra information about what is being watched and related websites, using TV, PC and mobiles. Depending on the viewers' needs, that extra information may be viewed immediately, stored for later view or pushed to other device. Each device maintains awareness of each other and are able to: move interaction to the device that makes the most sense in a specific context, use several devices simultaneously, and use the mobile device as a remote to the TV and PC. Limitations include: the system relies almost exclusively on social networks to receive and share content, for interaction and dialogues; and the limited viewer direct influence on the new contents presented as extra information. Our work is more flexible in these concerns. 2BEON [12], currently called WeOnTVis, an iTV application which supports the communication between viewers, textually and in real time, while watching a specific program. It also allows viewers to see which of their contacts are online, which programs they are watching, and instant messaging on the iTV, demonstrated to be important to give viewers a sense of presence and was implemented with smartphones as "secondary input devices". This work demonstrates the importance of sharing information with viewers' contacts about what they are watching on TV, which supports our own decision of including a sharing functionality in eiTV. Cronkite [13] provides extra information to viewers of broadcast news. While viewers are watching a news story, they feel the need to know more about it, they press the "interest" button on their remote and the system provides them with extra information on the computer display. The extra information, is about the story that they are watching rather than specific topics of interest inside the story, which is somehow limited. To have the system working, both TV and PC need to be simultaneously on. The system is limited considering that the extra information is not stored for latter view (and that might be the viewers' preference). Our application stores the related information for later use, the simultaneous use of iTV and PC is a possibility but not the only option, viewers may select very specific topics of interest inside a story instead of the whole story and some specific functionalities, as asynchronous communication tools, were also contemplated.

3 Crossmedia Design Challenges

This section describes the key aspects, cognitive and affective, that need to be considered to effectively design crossmedia environments and interfaces, with a special focus on the design challenges associated with video and different devices.

Media and Cognition: Norman's view [14] defines two fundamental cognitive modes. The experiential mode allows us to perceive and react to events naturally and without cognition, but require different technological support, and the medium affects the way we interpret and use the message and its impact on us. To exemplify, TV and video are typically watched in an experiential mode while learning strongly relies on reflection. A successful integration of media should have into account what each medium and device is most suited for in each context of use, augmenting and complementing their capabilities in a flexible combination.

Crossmedia Interaction, Conceptual Model and User Experience: The main challenges of crossmedia interaction design described by [15] include: consistency, interoperability, and technological literacy needed for the different devices. The conceptual model, how the software will look like and act, is also a very important aspect since several interaction scenarios and contexts are involved [16]. The quality of the interaction cannot be measured only by the quality of the system parts, but as a whole. In this context, the user experience (UX) may be evaluated through how well it supports the synergic use of each medium and the different kinds of affordances involved, also understanding what makes the user pass the current medium boundaries to use other media as well. According to [17], the UX may involve the isolated perception of the medium (distributed), one of the biggest barriers to its efficient use and adoption, or the perception of the system as a whole unity (coherent). According to [10], the UX evaluation methods and measures relevant, when ubiquitous TV is involved, are: physiological data; data mining, log files, observation, case studies, lab experiments, experience sampling method, probes, diaries, interviews, surveys and focus groups. The combination of methods to use depends on each specific case.

Supporting Crossmedia HCI: In this context, the migration of tasks is supported via crossmedia usability and continuity, influencing on how well and smoothly users' skills and experiences are transferred across the different devices [18] and contexts of use. The consistent look and feel across media is an important requirement, even if it should not limit the goal of having each medium doing what it is most suited for and extending its characteristics (synergic use) [19].

Designing for Different Devices and Contexts of Use: Crossmedia design involves designing interfaces for different devices. To understand the devices, and have each device doing what it is most suited for, the best approach is usually to study each particular situation, including device characteristics and cognitive and affective aspects associated to its use: why people use them, in which mode, compare them, etc., and the design guidelines for each device [8] followed by an adequate combination.

4 Crossmedia Design in eiTV

In brief, this Section presents main functionalities and design options concerning the eiTV Crossmedia system, in response to the challenges identified in Sect. 3.

4.1 eiTV Architecture

The eiTV system is a portal aggregator of all the functionalities which may be accessed from any of the devices (iTV, PC and mobile phones) thus working as a true 'ecosystem of devices' in a client-server architecture. Through the portal we may: generate web contents; see, edit and share web contents (with persons with or without a portal account), upload files, change profile, etc. In sum, everyone may receive web contents generated by the eiTV, a characteristic that provides **flexibility** to the application.

4.2 Flexible Navigation Model

We opted for a menu style navigation which provides **users** much more **control** over their choices, considering that all the functionalities may be accessed at any moment, directly through the menu or through the chromatic keys. This model improves: the application **interoperability** since it shows people how it works (what functions it supports and how); the **user experience** which becomes more **coherent** considering that users easily perceive the system as a whole unit; the **crossmedia interaction continuity** through different devices and the **interaction consistency** considering that it becomes easier to reuse users interaction knowledge. Due to its **flexibility** this model is also more adapted to changes **in cognition modes,** levels of **attention** and technological **literacy.** As to the interfaces they are simpler, have a minimalist aesthetic and were designed based on each device characteristics and the guidelines.

4.3 eiTV Functionalities

a) The **Create** central functionality allows users to watch videos and select topics of interest for further information. The information available about the video differs in focus and scope (video content and video Meta-info). Both types of information were made available on the three proposed *levels of information,* from less to high informative: level 1 (topics) only implies the use of the *OK* button in order to select topics of interest; level 2 (summary) implies the immediate display of extra information as a brief summary about the topics (overlaid or embedded onscreen); level 3 (structured) implies the immediate display of extra information, namely a structured list of that topic main aspects or options that the user may choose from (overlaid or embedded onscreen). At any moment, the user can change between levels of information by pressing button 1, 2 or 3 or by using the directional buttons or by using the mouse or touch screen (depending on the device being used to create the web content). Thus, the eiTV navigation is adaptable to users with different technological **literacy**. It was decided to maintain the 3 levels of information, with embedded and overlaid options on levels 2 and 3, since we saw from the previous prototypes, that they play an important role to accommodate viewers' changes in **cognition modes**, levels of **attention**, **goals**, **needs** and interaction **preferences**.

- WebContent: My input
- Each web content is organized as follows. The left side menu contains all the topics selected by the user, presented by the order of selection in the video, to improve contextualization, but the user may choose to see them by alphabetical or logical (content dependent) order (see Fig. 1a). Sub-categories of the topics are presented in the top menu. The web content is presented inside a 'portal' which also has all the other functionalities: Create, Search, Share, Profile and DF. The Search functionality also allows the upload of information to a specific web content. Thus, bellow the selected topics presented on the left side menu, there is the 'My input' place where all the manually uploaded information is stored (text, pictures, etc.) (see Fig. 1b). This option was designed to take advantage of each **device characteristics** in order to provide **flexibility**.

Fig. 1. eiTV Web content Interface. Three types to organize all the selected topics (a); My input place in the web content (b); one of the web content editing possibilities (c)

- WebContent: editing
- Each web content has the possibility to be edited. This edition ranges from *uploading* textual information (if through the TV set) or textual information and files (if through PC or mobile devices) or GPS coordinates (if through the mobile), to *delete* the web content, a topic of the web content, a category from a specific topic or even just a simple paragraph (see Fig. 1c). This option was designed to provide users with **flexibility**, **control**, **autonomy**, **consistent interaction** and to take advantage of each **device characteristics** and **user experience**.
- WebContent: Contextualizing
- **Continuity** and **contextualization** (see Fig. 2) was supported via the use of some excerpts from the original video, namely the excerpts that were being watched in the moment of the topic selection. By default, when reaching the web content, users are positioned in the first chosen topic and the first thing that they see is the excerpt of the video that was being watched when the topic was selected (option 1 includes the video playing and option 2 includes the video paused). With these two options, we expected to gain a better understanding of which one is the preferred option to help creating a smooth transition with a good **contextualization**. On previous evaluations a third option relying on the presentation of a picture from the moment of the topic selection was made available. However, considering that it was the less appreciated option, it was not implemented this time.

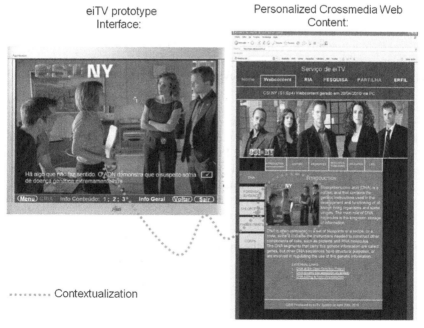

Fig. 2. Contextualization in crossmedia navigation

b) The **Search functionality** allows searching videos based on different criteria. Video criteria: title, actor name, etc.; and system criteria: video with or without web content(s) already generated. The found videos are presented in a table which let users know the video title, series, episode number, if the video is in the BOX, if the video is available through VOD and if a web content was already generated. By choosing one of these videos, users will be presented with the video synopsis and choose between watching the video, editing the web content (if there is one) or simply going back. This provides **flexibility** to the system.

c) The **Share** functionality is activated only after users accessed the Create or Search functionalities. This makes sense considering that viewers could not share something that was not yet created or found. The share functionality allows sharing the generated web content or retrieved video (with or without web content), with their contacts. On this functionality **flexibility** and **error prevention** were improved.

d) The User **Profile** functionality allows to upload users' personal data from their social network thus helping users with less **technological literacy**; allows to validate the input information; present clear and unequivocal error messages; consider all possibilities (forgot the PIN or password, need to create a new account, etc.). Considering that users do not like to input too much written information, the number of items to fill in are reduced to the minimum possible (name, sex, age, e-mails, mobile number, etc.). The user profile information is used to personalize the web content, thus improving **flexibility**. The login feature (designed based on each **device characteristics**) was also adapted to the access from PCs and mobile devices in a uniform and consistent way. In a web interface to have just a PIN number (as it happens on TV) is not enough. Thus, in order to assure a secure access in a uniform and consistent way, when accessing the portal through these devices, the viewer will be asked to enter an e-mail and a PIN number.

e) The **DF** functionality was designed to have each device doing what it is most suited for. In order to achieve this goal, contexts of use, device characteristics and cognitive and affective aspects associated to the devices use, were studied. In the case of mobile devices functionalities, the following were made available:

- *Great flexibility and mobility* (use it everywhere, anytime, anyway):
  When using the TV, the scroll is not an option, but that does not happen when using the other devices; contrary to TV and PC, mobile devices may be used everywhere, even when users are standing up, mining that any extra time may be used (if waiting for a medical appointment, in a bus queue, while in the train, etc.);
- *Location-based search using the GPS functionality*:
  the search functionality allows users to search videos related to their current location. As an example, when near the liberty statue the user may use this functionality to search, from its own system and the internet, videos related to that specific spot (this type of video files need to be inserted when using iTV or PC) (see Fig. 3);

- *Add immediately, or latter, shot pictures or videos,* that may be *related,* to the video being watched, as additional information to the web content or, instead, really integrated as part of the web content.

These functionalities provide the system with **flexibility**.

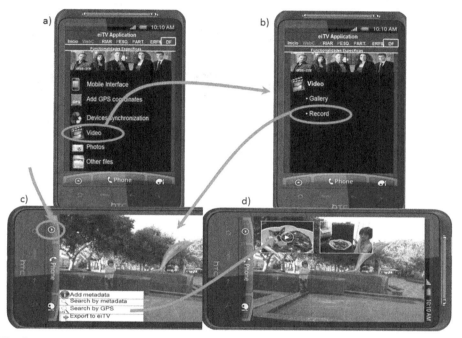

Fig. 3. Search videos and images from GPS coordinates. Video capture and location-based search: a) Options available at the DF functionality and 'Video' option being activated; b) Possibility to choose from a video gallery or to record a new video. The viewer choice was to record a new video; c) The viewer is choosing to search related videos and images by GPS coordinates; d) The two results – one video and one photo recorded in very close places - appear as thumbnails embedded in the video just recorded. A simple click on the video allows to watch it.

f) The **Devices Synchronization** functionality - The possibility to synchronize devices was designed and implemented in order to allow the application to work as a true ecosystem of devices. Figure 4 illustrates this option via mobile phone. When accessed through PC and TV, the same interfaces are available. Only the interface presented in Fig. 4a) changes considering that 'Add GPS coordinates' is a mobile phone specific option.

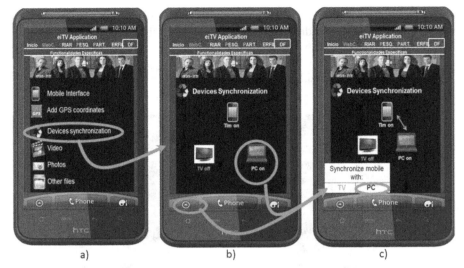

a)   b)   c)

Fig. 4. eiTV Devices Synchronization. Synchronizing devices: a) Options available at the DF functionality and 'Devices Synchronization' option being selected; b) Automatic detection on the connected interfaces. Viewer use the phone button in order to activate the menu to choose to which device synchronize his mobile; c) In this case is choosing PC (the only device on).

Consistency in UX and the perception of the system as a whole coherent unity independently of the device being used was also a priority. In spite of having considered the mobile device characteristics and contexts of use in the design, towards a more simplified design, we decided to keep a coherent layout in terms of colours, symbols and other graphic elements, as navigational buttons, in order to better contextualize users, give them a sense of unity in their UX and to allow a smooth transition among media and devices. This way, it was possible to provide users with a sense of sequence and continuity, respect the context of use and be consistent in terms of look and feel and navigational options in all the devices, and to help the perception of the application as a unity. Users are aware that they may access their eiTV system through different devices whenever they create web contents, helping to conceptually understand the system as an 'ecosystem of devices'. An example of the resulting design interface is presented in Fig. 5.

— — Visual feedback of the viewer choice   ▪ ▪ ▪ ▪ ▪ (Crossmedia) link to generated web content

Fig. 5. eiTV Mobile Interface *Create* functionality (a); topics selection interface with the information level 2 activated (b); aditional information immediately presented when a topic is selected by the user and the information level 2 is activated (c); interface to the addition of files captured on the moment to the web content being created (d); interface of the generated web content, based on the users selected topics (b–e)

5   Evaluation

The UX evaluation methods and measures considered relevant for this specific case as a final evaluation were: observation, case studies, lab experiments, experience sampling method, questionnaires, interviews and focus groups. The evaluation process started with a demonstration of the high-fidelity prototype using all the three devices involved (iTV, PC and mobile) and all the functionalities. Then, users were asked to perform tasks that allowed using all the eiTV functionalities (central and devices specific ones), through the prototype in five different contextual scenarios, and devices, with transitions between them. At a simulated 'living room' environment, Users started using the prototype, by generating two different web contents, first through iTV, and next through PC. The web content 1 was created through TV and edited/personalized via TV; web content 2 was created via PC and edited/personalized via TV. Next, they moved to the school bar and edited and personalized the web contents 1 and/or 2 via mobile. Next, they generated web content 3 through mobile while seated at the school bar. Then, they moved to the school backyard, created a video, and searched related videos by GPS coordinates (*Location-based search using the GPS functionality*) which were added to the web content to personalize it. Then, they entered the school and, at the lobby, used the mobile to take a picture, add the metadata manually, and add the picture to the web content. Next, they moved to the bar and, standing up at the end of the bar queue (like other public queues), they personalized the web content with their GPS coordinates. Next, they moved to the library that, although surrounded by people, is a quiet place (context like a medical clinic waiting room) to view the final web contents. Finally, they moved to the 'living room' and viewed the three final web contents using all the devices. Note that during the changes of context, the luminosity conditions, as well as the surround conditions (noise), changed when going from the building interior to the exterior, and vice versa. The interaction with the GUI high-fidelity prototype occurred via the three devices. It is important to mention that the evaluation process took place in real contexts of use, one of the most important factors to consider when testing crossmedia environments.

Finally, viewers were asked to fill a questionnaire and were interviewed. The questionnaire was based on the USE questionnaire (usefulness, satisfaction and ease of use) [20]; the NASA TLX questionnaire (cognitive overload) [21]; and usability heuristics. There were 90 participants, ranging from 18 to 65 years old, which were grouped into 3 evaluation groups: group 1 (G1) composed of 30 students aged between 18 and 25; group 2 (G2) composed of 30 persons aged between 25 and 45 and group 3 (G3) composed of 30 persons aged between 45 and 65. Inside each group the participants were categorized as follows: 10 with high technological literacy; 10 with medium technological literacy and 10 with poor technological literacy. No one ever participated on previous evaluations. As to the participants technological literacy categorization, it was possible via the use of a questionnaire with questions as: do you use Internet? e-mail? Facebook? How many hours a day? From which devices? Do you have a smartphone? Which functionalities do you use on your smartphone? etc.

Results are presented next. Independently of the group (and thus, age), medium and high technological literacy categories reacted well to difficulties. However, when considering low technological literacy categories, it was possible to see that, in the presence of difficulties, G3 reacted with higher resistance and discouragement than G2 and G1. In what relates to the iTV interaction, G2 and G3 were the ones with higher facility, which is visible by the results presented on Table 1, where we can also see the preferred devices to generate the web content. As expected, the older generation prefers the iTV to generate the web content (60%), while G2 prefers the PC and the youngest prefer the mobile. This may be explained by an increase in the use of cable TV options and applications as Netflix. Thus, older generations are becoming more and more used to interact even through iTV while younger generations, in spite being very used to interact, are becoming very distant from iTV (due to a change in their video consumption habits which are traditionally mobile based).

In what relates to the preferred devices to access and personalize the web content we can see from Table 2 that the mobile device was the preferred in all groups. In spite preferring the iTV to generate the web content, the older group (G3) prefers the mobile to access and personalize it thus clearly valuing the mobility that a smartphone brings to the system.

Table 1. Preferred device to generate the web content

Device to generate the Web content	G1	G2	G3
iTV	20%	37%	**60%**
PC	43%	**50%**	33%
Mobile	**37%**	13%	7%

Table 2. Preferred device to access and personalize the Web Content

Device to access de Web Content	G1	G2	G3
iTV	0%	7%	**13%**
PC	10%	10%	27%
Mobile	**90%**	**83%**	**60%**

In terms of information level, more users preferred level 1 (the less intrusive and less informational) if from mobile, level 2 is the preferred from iTV and level 3 is the preferred from PC. This result stresses an increase in users preference to select additional info to access later on when they are watching video on PC and iTV. These results are contrary to previous studies, which revealed that the preferred level for interaction was on the move with a mobile, when compared with.

TV or PC, where users preferred not to interrupt a more experiential mode of watching videos. These results, which are in accordance with the ones presented on Table 1, may indicate a changing in paradigm, and that independently of the device being used users are becoming more and more used to interact, even when through iTV. One explanation may be the fact that the information level 2 is very similar to the Video on Demand and/or Netflix synopsis option.

In terms of specific mobile devices functionalities, namely, the '*Location-based search using the GPS functionality*' and the '*Add immediately, or latter, shot pictures or videos*' the results of the evaluation are presented on Table 3.

Table 3. Evaluation of specific mobile devices functionalities

	G1	G2	G3
Useful	94%	90%	91%
Easy to use	97%	93%	91%
Easy to learn	97%	92%	83%
Like to have it	99%	94%	87%
Recommend to a friend	98%	90%	91%

As somehow expected, G1 was the group more enthusiastic with these functionalities. It makes sense if considering that the youngest population is the one that spends more hours per day using mobile devices. G2 results were slightly lower. As to G3, the results were even lowest but not so low as expected, which is a good indicator that this group has facility to adapt to mobile devices functionalities.

As to the *Devices Synchronization* functionality it was considered useful (G1: 97%; G2: 91%; G3: 98%) and easy to use (G1: 98%; G2: 93%; G3: 97%) in all the groups which is a very good indicator.

It is important to mention that the intention of transmitting a sense of unity was achieved: G1: 93%; G2: 87%; G3: 73% and, in general, 93% of the users referred that they immediately felt "inside" the same application, despite using different devices. As a whole the eiTV crossmedia system was evaluated as presented on Table 4.

Table 4. Overall evaluation of the whole eiTV crossmedia

Whole application	G1	G2	G3
Useful	93%	90%	70%
Easy to use	87%	83%	63%
Easy to learn	83%	80%	63%
Like to have it	93%	87%	67%
Recommend to a friend	97%	93%	83%

As can be seen, the evaluation of groups G1 and G2 are very close which was somehow expected. This indicates that the G1 has higher propensity to the use of (specific) technology, due to their young age, is bridged by G2 years of technology use experience. As to the G3 results they are very good if considering that is the oldest group and the worst obtained classification was 63% meaning that 19 out of 30 persons found the system easy to use and easy to learn. In spite a good start, a lot must be done in terms of Interfaces design research to adjust them to older populations.

6   Conclusions and Future Work

The evaluation results were very encouraging. In many aspects, the designed functionalities and the system flexibility were perceived as useful and an added value in the crossmedia research area. Some design options allowed to accommodate the changes in users' cognitive mode (e.g., information levels), and the prototype was designed and tested in real mobile scenarios and contexts of use. Considering the design framework followed, the trends in the use of multiple devices, and the results of this and previous studies, we have reasons to believe that our goal for this crossmedia context is worth pursuing and that we can achieve quite good results with all the devices in different scenarios. As future work, we intend to explore the devices technological advances to create new functionalities capable to better support users needs and different cognitive modes. A continuous improvement of the interfaces, so they may become easier to learn and adopted by an elderly population, is also a goal.

Acknowledgments. This work is partially supported by FCT through LASIGE Multiannual Funding and the ImTV research project (UTA-Est/MAI/0010/2009). To Diogo Silva, for his collaboration in the development of the first generation eiTV prototypes.

References

1. Gambarato, R.: Crossmedia, Multimedia and Transmdia. Published on 20 of October 2020. https://www.youtube.com/watch?v=G3wdbajO6js. Accessed 30 Nov 2020
2. Moloney, K.: Multimedia, Crossmedia, Tranmedia... What's in a name? Published on 21 of April 2014. https://transmediajournalism.org/2014/04/21/multimedia-crossmedia-transm edia-whats-in-a-name/. Accessed 30 Nov 2020
3. Jenkins, H.: Transmedia Missionaries: Henry Jenkins. Published in 23 of July 2009. http://www.youtube.com/watch?v=bhGBfuyN5gg. Accessed 19 Nov 2020
4. Prata, A., Chambel, T.: Mobility in crossmedia systems, the design challenges that need to be addressed. In: Abásolo, M.J., Kulesza, R., PinaAmargós, J.D. (eds.) jAUTI. CCIS, vol. 1202, pp. 67–86. Springer, Cham (2020). https://doi.org/10.1007/978-3-030-56574-9_5
5. Prata, A., Chambel, T.: Mobility in a crossmedia environment capable of generating person-alized informal learning contents from iTV, PC and mobile devices. In: Proceedings of JAUTI 2019 – VIII Conferência Iberoamericana sobre Aplicações e Usabilidade da TV Interativa, Rio de Janeiro, Brasil, pp. 59–71 (2019)
6. Bonometti, S.: Learning in cross-media environment. Int. J. Web-Based Learn. Teach. Technol. **12**(4), 48–57 (2017). https://doi.org/10.4018/IJWLTT.2017100105
7. Taplin, J.: Long time coming: has interactive TV finally arrived?. Opening keynote. In: Pro-ceedings of 9th European Conference on Interactive TV and Video: Ubiquitous TV (EuroiTV 2011), in coop with ACM, Lisbon, Portugal, p. 9 (2011)
8. Prata, A., Chambel, T.: Going beyond iTV: designing flexible video-based cross-media inter-active services as informal learning contexts. In: Proceedings of 9th European Con-ference on Interactive TV and Video: Ubiquitous TV (EuroiTV 2011), in coop with ACM, Lisbon, Portugal, pp. 65–74 (2011)
9. Pemberton, L., Fallahkhair, S.: Design Issues for Dual Device Learning: interactive televi-sion and mobile phone. In: Proceedings of 4th World Conference on mLearning - Mobile Technology: The Future of Learn in Your Hands (mLearn 2005), Cape Town, South Africa (2005)
10. Obrist, M., Knoch, H.: How to investigate the quality of user experience for ubiquitous TV?. Tutorial. In: Proceedings of EuroiTV 2011, 9th European Conference on Interactive TV and Video: Ubiquitous TV, Lisbon, Portugal (2011)
11. Martin, R., Holtzman, H.: Newstream. A multi-device, cross-medium, and socially aware app-roach to news content. In: Proceedings of 8th European Interactive TV Conference (EuroiTV 2010), in coop with ACM, Tampere, Finland, pp. 83–90 (2010)
12. Abreu, J.: Design de Serviços e Interfaces num Contexto de Televisão Interactiva. Doctoral thesis, Aveiro University, Aveiro, Portugal (2007)
13. Livingston, K., Dredze, M., Hammond, K., Birnbaum, L.: Beyond broadcast. In: Proceedings of ACM IUI 2003, The Seventh International Conference on Intelligent User Interfaces, Miami, USA, 12–15 January 2003, pp. 260–262 (2003)

14. Norman, D.: Things that Make us Smart. Addison Wesley Publishing Company, Reading (1993)
15. Segerståhl, K.: Utilization of pervasive IT compromised? Understanding the adoption and use of a cross media system. In: Proceedings of 7th International Conference on Mobile and Ubiqitous Multimedia (MUM 2008) in cooperation with ACM SIGMOBILE, Umea, Sweden, pp. 168–175 (2008)
16. Norman, D.: The Design of Everyday Things. Basic Books, New York (2002)
17. Segerståhl, K., Oinas-Kukkonen, H.: Distributed user experience in persuasive technology environments. In: de Kort, Y., IJsselsteijn, W., Midden, C., Eggen, B., Fogg, B.J. (eds.) PERSUASIVE 2007. LNCS, vol. 4744, pp. 80–91. Springer, Heidelberg (2007). https://doi.org/10.1007/978-3-540-77006-0_10
18. Florins, M., Vanderdonckt, J.: Graceful degradation of user interfaces as a design method for multiplatform systems. In: Proceedings of the ACM International Conference on Intelligent User Interfaces (IUI 2004), Funchal, Madeira, pp. 140–147 (2004)
19. Nielsen, J.: Coordinating User Interfaces for Consistency. Neuauflage 2002 ed. The Morgan Kaufmann Series in Interactive Technologies, San Francisco (1989)
20. Lund, A.: Measuring Usability with the USE Questionnaire. https://garyperlman.com/quest/quest.cgi?form=USE. Accessed 15 Oct 2020
21. NASA: NASA TLX Paper and Pencil Version. https://humansystems.arc.nasa.gov/groups/tlx/tlxpaperpencil.php. Accessed 01 Oct 2020

Teledu: Transmedia Learning Ecosystem for People at Risk of Exclusion

Carlos de Castro Lozano[1]([envelope]) [iD], José Miguel Ramírez Uceda[1],
Beatriz Sainz de Abajo[2] [iD], Enrique García Salcines[1] [iD], Jon Arambarri Basañez[3] [iD],
Joaquín Aguilar Cordón[1], Javier Cabo Salvador[1] [iD], and Francisco Alcantud Marín[4] [iD]

[1] University of Cordoba, CITEC Campus de Rabanales, 14012 Córdoba, Spain
malcaloc@uco.es
[2] University of Valladolid, Paseo de Belén, 15, 47011 Valladolid, Spain
[3] European University of the Atlantic, Calle Isabel Torres, 21, 39011 Santander, Spain
[4] University of Valencia, Avenida de Blasco Ibáñez, 13, 46010 València, Spain

Abstract. The TELEDU tele-education ecosystem, integrated by software and hardware components, allows the use of Web resources through *Interactive Digital TV* (iDTV) without the need to be continuously connected. It works with any existing digital TV standard and is especially useful for users who do not have broadband, being a very effective solution in places where there is a digital divide. The user must have, at least, a cell phone with 3G connection and any of these three options: *Digital Terrestrial TV* (DTT), Satellite TV or Cable TV. The conception of TELEDU is based on the premise that the software will offer a friendly interaction. Based on this, an interoperable, open and scalable environment has been developed, which works with PCs, tablets, smartphones and digital TV, offering a visual interface oriented to children, the elderly and people with functional diversity and people with technophobia. The concept of *Transmedia Online Object Content* (TOOC) is introduced, so that digital contents are in different formats and people with functional diversity and people with technophobia. The concept of TOOC is introduced, so that digital contents are in different formats (paper book, e-book, post, audio, interactive video, virtual reality, serious game, webinar, etc.), on different devices and platforms, locally or in the cloud, with usable multimodal access designed for everyone, and adapting to each user, regardless of the accessibility problems they have.

Keywords: *Interactive Digital TV* (iDTV) · Hybrid IPTV ·
Transmedia-Learning platform (Tm-Learning) · *Massive Open Online Course*
(MOOC) · Extended reality · Learning objects · Interactivity · Usability ·
Accessibility · Gamification · *Transmedia Open Object Content* (TOOC)

1 Introduction

In recent times, there has been a paradigm shift in the consumption of content, mainly by the new generations. Internet users and mobile devices have grown exponentially, as has the viewing of videos and photos on social networks. Seventy percent of the

© Springer Nature Switzerland AG 2021
M. J. Abásolo et al. (Eds.): jAUTI 2020, CCIS 1433, pp. 105–115, 2021.
https://doi.org/10.1007/978-3-030-81996-5_8

world's population has a cell phone with a minimum data connection. The number of households with access to television services has also increased. In 2018, the number of households watching television through one of the existing platforms exceeded 1.6 billion. In addition, forecasts point to a gradual increase in this figure, to over 1.7 billion in 2023[1].

Despite well-known and controversial initiatives by technology corporations to increase connectivity in the global South, such as Facebook's *Free Basics* [1], there are still millions of users without Internet access. This exacerbates inequalities and their integral development. It is therefore necessary to focus on reducing the digital divide in the long term [2]. This gap has a special impact on education. Not all students can access the Internet to follow the school course, nor do all those who do have access do so under equal conditions[2].

The Covid-19 pandemic has brought about major changes in schools and in the way teacher-student communication takes place. According to a study by Empantallados[3] and GAD[4], with support from the European Commission, one out of every two families has bought an electronic device for their children's online classes. The Universidad Internacional de La Rioja (UNIR) highlights a 900% worldwide growth in online training since 2000[5].

During the confinement, schools and universities broadcast their classes by videostreaming, using Zoom, Meet, etc., increasing the use of e-Learning platforms such as Moodle, and access to video MOOCs. Only families with broadband WiFi or 4G data flat rate have been able to access.

To avoid the digital divide among families who do not have broadband Internet at home and considering that television has become the most important means of communication in the house, governments and universities are called upon to propose alternatives that allow access to digital content. In this way, by encouraging the use of television, educational programs based on high quality interactive videos have been proposed.

Many countries, in order to solve the problem, have created educational TV channels to broadcast classes via DTT, cable or via satellite, aimed at families with scarcely any economic resources. Unlike those who have broadband Internet at home, these families have not been able to access an e-Learning platform and, therefore, did not work interactively and collaboratively with the rest of the students and teachers.

Moreover, thinking about users without broadband access, but who have television and a mobile device with 3G access, the TELEDU ecosystem was developed. A preliminary lecture of the work has been presented at the ninth Iberoamerican Conference on Applications and Usability of Interactive Television, jAUTI 2020. This paper elaborates

---

[1] https://es.statista.com/estadisticas/600298/numero-de-hogares-con-television-a-nivel-mundial/.

[2] https://www.unicef.es/educa/blog/covid-19-brecha-educativa.

[3] https://empantallados.com/.

[4] https://gad3.com/estudio-de-empantallados-y-gad3-el-impacto-de-las-pantallas-en-los-hogares-espanoles-durante-el-confinamiento-d17/.

[5] https://www.unir.net/actualidad/internacional/por-que-triunfa-el-sistema-de-educacion-universitaria-on-line-en-espana-y-colombia-replica-su-modelo/.

and shows more extensively the scope of the development and evaluation of the usability of the training platform.

2 Background

2.1 Hybrid IPTV

Unlike analog television, *Integrated Digital Television* (iDTV) allows incorporating, in addition to the audio/video signal, a data signal through which applications (software) travel to the viewers' receivers or *Set-Top-Box* (STB). These can interact with the program transmitter (the television station), as well as the alternative of broadcasting the same contents through interactive IPTV broadcasting systems.

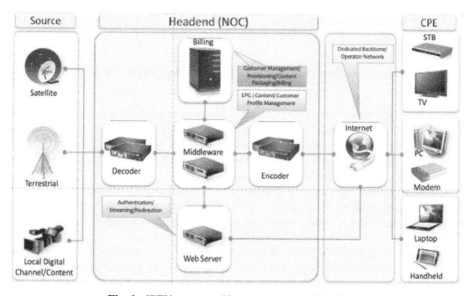

Fig. 1. IPTV system achitecture. Source: SlideShare.

Although different standards have emerged globally for the broadcasting of television, hybrid IPTV[6] (Fig. 1) is the solution to these problems of global standardization of iDTV.

The hybrid set-top box allows content from a variety of sources, including terrestrial broadcast, satellite and cable, to be combined with video delivered over the Internet via an Ethernet connection on the device.

This makes it easier for viewers to access a wider variety of content on their TVs, without the need for a separate box for each service. Hybrid IPTV set-top boxes also allow users to access a range of advanced interactive services, such as VOD/catch-up

---

[6] https://es.qaz.wiki/wiki/Internet_Protocol_television.

TV, as well as Internet applications, including video telephony, surveillance, gaming, shopping, e-government, etc., through a TV set.

Low-income households, because it depends on a flat monthly fee, cannot enjoy the hybrid IPTV broadband standard. However, most of these families, even the poorest, have a cell phone with 3G and free access to DTT, satellite TV or cable TV.

Hybrid Broadcast Broadband TV (HbbTV) is an initiative that seeks to harmonize IPTV broadcasting, broadband and entertainment content delivery through smart TV sets connected to set-top boxes. It can be considered a hybrid IPTV technology alternative to SmartTV technology [3, 4]. While SmartTV requires downloading different applications to access the information it offers, with HbbTV technology there is no need to download anything. Just press a button on the remote control and a menu will be automatically displayed on the TV. In June 2018, three major Spanish platforms, the publicly owned Radio y Televisión Española, S. A. (RTVE) and privately owned Atresmedia and Mediaset España joined forces to launch officially the LOVEStv service, based on HbbTV, which is completely free for users and will seek to become a new evolution of free-to-air television.

2.2 Transmedia Learning Platform and Transmedia Interactive Learning Objects

Transmedia, interactive, accessible, gamified, usable and adaptive contents, which can be easily produced by the teacher or the student with different authoring tools [5], based on the use of serious games, are now needed and are more effective and are increasingly in demand. It has been proven that with them the student's participation in the learning process is more intense and effective.

Virtual and augmented reality systems and immersive systems are proliferating. Large companies (Facebook, Google, Apple, Microsoft) are betting heavily on these technologies. In the near future, everyone will be producing digital content for these devices.

The success of MOOCs [6], invisible learning [7], new theories based on social constructivism [8], connectivism [9], flipped Learning 3.0[7], adaptive ubiquitous learning [10] and intelligent assistants or chatboot[8] are latent in the new digital society. The use of these systems has a favorable impact, both in the decrease of the dropout rate and in the high acquisition of knowledge by students. This is the design-for-all approach.

More and more learners are using e-Learning systems, whether on computer, tablet or even mobile. Personalization through adaptive intelligent systems applications begins to be a necessity in the new way of access to knowledge after the Covid-19 crisis.

If we design new state-of-the-art digital contents and Authoring tools for the production of these contents, which integrate previous technologies and new learning models in a ubiquitous *Transmedia-Learning* (Tm-Learning) platform, we can achieve an online learning ecosystem that is more effective than the current systems.

---

[7] https://digscholarship.unco.edu/heflc/2017/schedule/2/.

[8] https://www.researchgate.net/publication/290472812_IEEEIBM_Watson_Student_Showcase.

With this in mind, the online learning ecosystem, TELEDU, was developed and a new concept of learning objects was defined: *Transmedia Open Online Content* (TOOCs[9]).

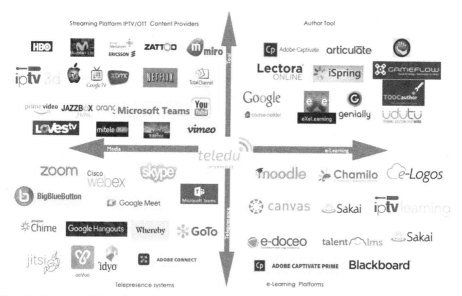

Fig. 2. Main providers of streaming, videoconferencing, Authoring tools and e-Learning platforms. Own source.

The most important key to take into account in a transmedia narrative is user participation through interactivity and gamification [11]. The role of the audience in transmedia storytelling is quite active. We must encourage them to participate and give them their own space to interact and contribute with comments and ideas. The implementation of game mechanics in non-game contexts leads to greater user participation [12].

The growth of *Over-The-Top* (OTT) Internet and mobile video streaming services is a major development in the distribution, transmission and consumption of global media sport [13]. During the Covid-19 pandemic, the use of IPTV/OTT systems [14], streaming video, authoring tools for content creation, and e-Learning platforms, live or *Video on Demand* (VOD), in the different social networks (Youtube Live, Vimeo, Facebook Live, Twitter, Periscope, Instagram), for entertainment, *webinars* and online classes has increased (see Fig. 2). These technologies have favored the exponential growth of iDTV systems, whether on the computer, tablet or even the cell phone.

3   Methodology

This work has been divided into two stages: the development phase of the TELEDU ecosystem and the evaluation phase.

---

[9] https://www.oepm.es/es/signos_distintivos/resultados.html?denominacion=Contenga&texto=tooc&p=2.

3.1 TELEDU Development

TELEDU is the result of 20 years of research and development by more than 10 university groups from RedAUTI.

Because of the collaboration between the different agents, **a hybrid standard was created**. This standard integrates Ginga[10] (for IPTV services and the *Nipo-Brazilian Digital Terrestrial TV System* (ISDB-T$_B$)), and the European (*Hybrid Broadcast Broadband TV* (HbbTV)) and the Chinese (*Digital Terrestrial Multimedia Broadcast* (DTMB)) standards, with the SiestaCloud ecosystem, for the development of interactivity applications on *Internet Protocol Television* (IPTV) and *Digital Terrestrial Television* (DTT). All this considering the SIMPLIT usability standards and the accessibility of the *World Wide Web Consortium* (W3C).

The implementation of an authoring tool for the development of interactive DTT/IPTV applications was contemplated, under the concept of existing templates in open access repositories that would be an extension of the Unity framework, for the creation of 2D and 3D content, with easy-to-use extended reality. In this way, prosumers (producers + consumers) do not have to program a single line of code.

A methodology for the production of accessible, adaptive and standardized audiovisual material in the cultural, entertainment, educational and commercial context was also proposed [15].

The TELEDU model is a hybrid IPTV/OTT ecosystem that is composed of three components: technological, methodological and of evaluation:

1. **The technological component** covers the design and implementation of a ubiquitous online learning platform, with a usable and accessible interface for interactive digital television (IPTV Learning) and the development of the Author tool, TOOC Author, for the creation of transmedia learning objects, open online.
2. **The methodological component** comprises the design and development of online learning models based on connectivist theories [9], flipped learning 3.0 and ubiquitous learning [10] in Tm-Learning platforms, using *Connective Massive Open Online Course* (cMOOC) interactives and serious games. In this methodological part, these components were analyzed and evaluated, taking into account the different learning theories and the ideas arising from the networked community.
3. **For the evaluation,** a testing stage has been proposed to guarantee both the quality and the effectiveness of the evaluation system model, the technology, and the contents or learning objects. These tests are of usability, accessibility and effectiveness in the learning levels achieved. For this purpose, several scenarios and models with students in formal training were considered.

3.2 Ecosystem Assessment

In order to test the effectiveness of the didactic models in the levels of learning achieved, the starting point was the definition of ubiquitous training models, in which different elements intervene: permanence, accessibility, immediacy, interactivity and adaptability [16, 17].

---

[10] http://www.ginga.org.br/es/sobre.

Once the models were defined, one was selected and we proceeded to the instructional design and content development in two subjects: Automatic Regulation, from the 3rd year of the Electrical Engineering Degree, and Integrated Production Systems, from the master's degree in Industrial Engineering, taught at the Superior Polytechnic School of the Universidad de Córdoba.

An evaluation system based on traditional MOOCs was proposed, using the Moodle platform, which served as a reference model to evaluate our proposed learning model, using the IPTV Learning platform and substituting MOOCs for TOOCs. The TELEDU proposal offers an evolution from MOOCs to TOOCs. A TOOC is a content, or transmedia learning object, open online, with a series of properties that identify it. It has to be gamified, interactive, usable, accessible and adaptive, designed for different types of devices and platforms (Smart TV, tablets, Smartphone, PC, VR glasses, e-books, etc.), complying with different standards (Scorm, SIMPLIT, W3C...).

For the evaluation process, the *"Sistema de Información y Atención al Usuario"* (SIAU) methodology was applied to a sample of 200 students in different academic courses.

In the first two months, the subject was taught in the traditional way. In the remaining two months, this methodology was applied with similar theoretical and practical contents.

An evaluation test was given at the end of each period. The results obtained by the students were measured and relationships were established between the results achieved with the proposed model and those achieved using a traditional pre-classroom or online course. The results showed that 95% of the students had learned much more with the TELEDU model and had had fun, although they had also worked harder. The difference in grades was evident. In the first exam, 48% of the students passed, while in the second exam, 95% passed.

To test the effectiveness of the model, usability (SIMPLIT12 Seal), accessibility (W3C13) and effectiveness in the levels of learning achieved were tested, comparing with the results of traditional e-Learning system models, using the methodology for determining attributes and metrics in *Adaptive Educational Hypermedia Systems* (AEHS) based on learning styles [17].

Finally, the usability of the learning environment was assessed through the Jakob Nielsen[11] heuristic evaluation survey among students.

4   Results

4.1   TELEDU and TOOC Author Ecosystem

TELEDU is an ecosystem that integrates the latest technological trends in human-computer interfaces and ubiquitous computing systems, cloud computing, artificial intelligence, blockchain and multimodal systems of interaction by gestures, movement and voice, in addition to *Internet of Things* (IoT).

TELEDU (Fig. 3) is composed of hardware (computer, tablet, smartphone, *STB*) and software (SiestaOS 2020 operating system, the IPTV Learning platform, and the authoring tool TOOC Author). It is compatible with any type of input and output device,

---

[11] https://revistas.ucp.pt/index.php/gestaoedesenvolvimento/article/view/83/75.

state-of-the-art, including virtual reality glasses and gloves, video game devices, IoT sensors, etc. In addition, it can adapt to the various iDTV standards (ISDB-T, HbbTV, DTMB, etc.).

One of the recommendations of the ITU-T Telecommunication Study Groups indicates that digital content and multimedia applications intended to run on IPTV terminal devices should be platform-independent, so that content creators and providers do not have to develop specific applications for each existing platform and device. It has been taken into account in the development of the authoring tool TOOC Author.

TELEDU has TOOC Author, which is complemented by Genially[12], designed and created by graduates of the Universidad de Córdoba, which is made available to students and teachers, allowing them to easily produce a TOOC.

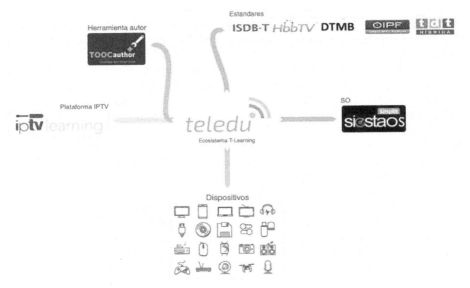

Fig. 3. Main providers of streaming, videoconferencing, authoring tools and e-Learning platforms. Own source.

4.2   Solution in Areas of Limited Bandwith Resources

The TELEDU ecosystem offers access to the IPTV Learning platform without the need for broadband WiFi at home.

Taking into account that, sometimes, families only have a TV with satellite or terrestrial connection, fed by a transmitter center for the educational TV channel, and a cell phone with 3G, a minimum equipment infrastructure has been designed to provide coverage.

---

[12] https://intef.es/wp-content/uploads/2019/03/Art%C3%ADculo-Genially-3.pdf.

This infrastructure consists of a STB decoder, a keyboard and a mouse (see Fig. 4). The STB is installed with the 2020 evolution of the SIeS-TAOS operating system, based on Ubuntu 2020, the Firefox Browser 83.0, the IPTV Learning platform, and the contents and resources according to the course(s) to be received.

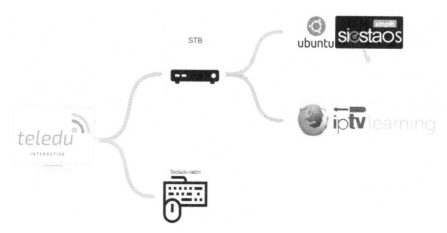

Fig. 4. Minimum hardware and software components of TELEDU. Own source.

4.3 Evaluation Resources Among the Surveyed Students

The most salient aspects that can be concluded from establishing the TELEDU methodology, which correspond to pedagogical interaction, test results, TOOCs quality assessment metrics, and learning styles test are:

1. Learners prefer visual and interactive content, especially videos, simulations, virtual reality, augmented reality and serious games. Interactive multimedia self-study learning objectives, with this type of digital content, are highly valued.
2. Eighty percent of the students only complete the activities and evaluable tasks, those that give them points to pass the course. If these activities are gamified, 98% of students have successfully completed the course.
3. Students learn more when they themselves are the ones who have to actively work on the lesson, search the Internet and provide resources and complementary information on the subject. It is when they become prosumers of information and knowledge (informal learning).
4. Students value positively the teacher who develops quality transmedia content, and negatively the one who just posted his notes and presentations in a *Learning Management System* (LMS). They also value positively the learning methodology based on critical thinking.
5. In fully online education, students' assignments must be very well planned. Follow-up should be continuous without reaching an exhaustive control by the teacher and giving a certain flexibility for the completion of the tasks and activities to be developed.

6. Students should feel that they are being tutored. The teacher must attend daily to questions, doubts or problems in a personal way, and to collective consultations through forums and videotutorials.
7. Students, in addition to the online activities, prefer to have a written reference guide, like a book, on the contents and methodology of the subject (transmedia).
8. Students prefer to use the latest technologies (virtual reality, augmented reality, immersive systems, serious-games, etc.). With regard to hardware, mobile touch-screen tablet systems, ultrabooks, IPTV, virtual and augmented reality glasses, are the most popular devices used to run a course (multi-device).
9. Synchronous systems (telepresence, chat, etc.) are not well accepted by learners if they are imposed on them. They prefer to use them according to their needs and not when the teacher plans it. They prefer to use telepresence and chats with the teacher for personal tutoring or among themselves.
10. Social networks are the incentive. They are used to it in their daily life (connectivism).

5 Conclusions

This paper presents TELEDU, designed as a learning model. It is based on critical thinking, connectivist and ubiquitous learning theories, as well as on adaptive transmedia learning objects based on serial games, which allows teachers and prosumers to create lessons with interactive audiovisual content and educational gamification systems, with feedback and scoring, facilitating the automation of student monitoring and evaluation.

By integrating software components, an iDTV ecosystem has been created, oriented to state-of-the-art e-learning processes. It has a fully usable interface (with SIMPLIT certification) for the iDTV based on the concept desktop.

The concept of transmedia, open, online, interactive, usable, accessible, adaptive and gamified (TOOC) content or learning object has been defined and created. TOOC Author has been designed and developed, integrated with the Gameflow Author tool, based on Unity, implementing these new learning objects in the IPTV Learning platform and achieving interoperability, usability and accessibility, which are key features for an application environment of this type, and agreed technical standards to enable such interoperability.

The module has been developed to integrate and embed in the IPTV Learning platform any application, tool or external Web platform. Any videoconferencing system or Web application, which is normally in use, can be integrated, although we cannot guarantee the usability and consistency of the system.

The effectiveness of the model has been tested through usability, accessibility and effectiveness tests on the learning levels achieved, comparing with the results of traditional e-Learning system models, through the SHAE methodology, based on learning styles.

A Tm-Learning IPTV/OTT for online learning called IPTV Learning has been developed and approved for occupational training in Spain and is in the process of approval in Chile.

Finally, a tool is being designed to convert the graphical user interfaces of external applications to the concept desktop interface, with SIMPLIT seal of usability.

References

1. Nothias, T.: Access granted: Facebook's free basics in Africa. Media, Cult. Soc. **42**, 329 (2020). https://doi.org/10.1177/0163443719890530
2. Instituto Nacional de Estadística y Geografía: Encuesta Nacional sobre Disponibilidad y Uso de Tecnologías de la Información en los Hogares (ENDUTIH). Inegi, pp. 1–18 (2019)
3. Zhao, X., Okamoto, T.: Adaptive multimedia content delivery for contextaware u-learning. Int. J. Mob. Learn. Organ. **5**, 46–63 (2011). https://doi.org/10.1504/IJMLO.2011.038691
4. Jaksic, B., Milosevic, I., Petrovic, M., Ilic, S., Bojanic, S., Vasic, S.: Characteristics of hybrid broadcast broadband television (HbbTV). Univ. Thought - Publ. Nat. Sci. **7**, 36–40 (2017). https://doi.org/10.5937/univtho7-14347
5. De Castro, C., et al.: Wiki tool for adaptive, accesibility, usability and colaborative hypermedia courses: Mediawikicourse (2011)
6. Al-Rahmi, W., Aldraiweesh, A., Yahaya, N., Bin Kamin, Y., Zeki, A.M.: Massive Open Online Courses (MOOCs): data on higher education. Data Br. **22**, 118–125 (2019). https://doi.org/10.1016/j.dib.2018.11.139
7. Moravec, J., Cobo, J.: Aprendizaje invisible. Hacia una nueva ecología de la educación. Razón y palabra, vol. 16 (2011)
8. Vall Castelló, B.: Bridging constructivism and social constructionism: the journey from narrative to dialogical approaches and towards synchrony. J. Psychother. Integr. **26**, 129–143 (2016). https://doi.org/10.1037/int0000025
9. Downes, S.: Connectivism and Connective Knowledge: essays on meaning and learning networks (2012)
10. Cope, B., Kalantzis, M.: Ubiquitous learning. Exploring the anywhere/anytime possibilities for learning in the age of digital media. In: Education Policy, vol. 264 (2009)
11. Merino Arribas, M.: El factor emocional en la narrativa transmedia y la televisión social. Fonseca J. Commun. **6**, 226–248 (2013)
12. Sainz de Abajo, B., De la Torre-Díez, I., López-Coronado, M., Aguiar Pérez, J., De Castro Lozano, C.: Aplicación plural de herramientas para gamificar. Análisis y comparativa. Presented at the 26 September 2019. https://doi.org/10.4995/inred2019.2019.10467
13. Hutchins, B., Li, B., Rowe, D.: Over-the-top sport: live streaming services, changing coverage rights markets and the growth of media sport portals. Media Cult. Soc. **41**, 975 (2019). https://doi.org/10.1177/0163443719857623
14. Li, S.C.S.: Television media old and new: a niche analysis of OTT, IPTV, and digital cable in Taiwan. Telemat. Inform. **34**, 1024–1037 (2017). https://doi.org/10.1016/j.tele.2017.04.012
15. La información digital actual, un nuevo modelo de contenido educativo para un entorno de aprendizaje ubicuo. RED. Rev. Educ. a Distancia. Unknown. 18–34 (2013)
16. El futuro de las tecnologías digitales aplicadas al aprendizaje de personas con necesidades educativas especiales. RED. Rev. Educ. a Distancia. 1–43 (2012). https://doi.org/10.13140/2.1.1853.5041
17. Leighton Álvarez, H., Prieto Ferraro, M., García Peñalvo, F.J.: Metodología para determinar atributos y métricas de calidad en sistemas hipermedia adaptativos educativos basados en estilos de aprendizaje. Rev. Educ. **29**, 91 (2011). https://doi.org/10.15517/revedu.v29i1.2026

iTV for the Elderly

TV Remote Control and Older Adults: A Systematic Literature Review

Daniel Carvalho[1,2]([✉]) [iD], Telmo Silva[1,2] [iD], and Jorge Abreu[1,2] [iD]

[1] Communication and Arts Department, University of Aveiro, Aveiro, Portugal
{daniel.carvalh,tsilva,jfa}@ua.pt
[2] CIC.DIGITAL/Digimedia, University of Aveiro, Aveiro, Portugal

Abstract. The remote control is a device normally used in conjunction with the TV-set, being this the preferred via of interaction. However, users like older adults frequently have difficulties using this device, due to the decrease in fine motor skills such as coordination of movements, grabbing objects, and also to memory and visual impairments. In this context, the present study presents a review of articles from the last five years, making it possible to understand in detail the difficulties of older adults in using the TV remote control, as well as to understand what solutions were found to overcome these difficulties. This review also made possible to understand how the physical interface of the remote control is composed and what operations and functions it is normally used for. The paper ends with a discussion that lists the general findings, also allowing to answer the objective imposed in this study. From the findings of the review, it is possible to understand the specific characteristics of older adults that emerge with aging, as well as the potential to improve the interface of the TV remote controls according to these characteristics, from simplifying the device interface, the redesign of its buttons, until the implementation of different input modalities such as voice commands and gestures.

Keywords: Older adult · Remote control · Interface

1 Introduction

The TV-set is currently found in most households, being the most used audio-visual device and one of the favourite technologies of the Portuguese population [1]. With the evolution of ICT's (Information and Communication Technologies), people started to encounter on the TV-set other types of features [2], such as notifications that appear on the screen [3] or contact other users through social networks [4]. To control these advanced features, it is normal to resort to the remote control, being a common electronic device that is part of everyday life [5]. Although this marriage between the TV-set and the remote control allows reaching a considerable part of the population, the use of this control device as the only form of interaction sometimes makes it difficult or even impossible for certain audiences to use some television applications, such as people with issues on fine motor skills [6]. Ouyang and Zhou [7] add that the increase in forms of

© Springer Nature Switzerland AG 2021
M. J. Abásolo et al. (Eds.): jAUTI 2020, CCIS 1433, pp. 119–133, 2021.
https://doi.org/10.1007/978-3-030-81996-5_9

interaction, functions, and multi-modal input methods on television generate exclusion of people like older adults, who have decreased perceptual, cognitive, and/or motor skills, as well as lack of experience in the use of new technologies. The authors of [8] corroborate this last statement, saying that modern products appear with more and more functions, making it difficult for older adults to use these products when they have physical and psychological restrictions. With regard to motor abilities, authors address that older adults have difficulties handling the TV remote control due to limitations in hand dexterity and precision, to perform tasks such as zapping on television [5, 9, 10]. Authors such as [11] and [5] also highlight the visual impairment of older adults, who have difficulties seeing small symbols, labels and other graphic elements that may exist on the remote control. Pereira [12], in his thesis "Princípios orientadores de design de interfaces para aplicações itv orientadas para seniores Portugueses" (translated from Portuguese as "Guiding principles of interface design for iTV applications targeted at Portuguese seniors"), addresses not only the reduction of the execution precision of movements in an older adult, but it also addresses the deterioration in the coordination of movements, causing older adults the need to look at the remote control to first interact and then look at the television screen to see the interface's reaction to the interaction made on the remote control. This implies the need to include animations and movement of graphic elements (as the focus highlight) from one point to another in a relatively slow way. This action, according to [12], allows the older adult user the time needed to shift their attention between the remote control and the television. In this context, older adults are one of the most important user groups for product designers, so during the interface design of the remote control it is mandatory to not only consider aesthetics issues, but also intuitive operation and interaction issues [13]. It is also important to consider older adults in the development of technologies for television, since the TV-set is the main technology of this user group for accessing information and entertainment [3]. Although there is already a good amount of research regarding the interaction of older adults with the TV, it is essential to demonstrate which are the most recent approaches to the use of the TV remote control by this target audience. Thus, it was made a review of the literature that addresses this field, whose findings are structured in 5 sections, allowing these: Provide clear knowledge about the older adults that participated in the reviewed studies; Understand the characteristics of the remote control; Identify the main problems that the physical and cognitive decline caused by aging causes in the use of the remote control; Understand how older adults often use the remote control; And what measures have been taken to help this population use or replace the remote control. At the end there will be a discussion regarding the results obtained, as well as to obtain the respective conclusions and perspectives for future work.

2   Method

A systematic review was carried out to find articles that make it possible to understand how the TV remote control is composed and the common difficulties in its use by the older adult population. For this review, the PRISMA Statement [14] was used. A review of articles written in English and Portuguese and published in the last 5 years (between 2016 and 2020) was carried out, being selected those that address, at least, the use of the

TV remote control. The results were subsequently filtered in order to find articles that address any user difficulties in using this interaction device. From this data processing, the conditions are provided to understand the type of interface used in the remote controls addressed in the observed studies, how the different authors characterize the use of the remote control by the older adult population, what are the main limitations that the authors encountered when older adults use the remote control and what possible solutions have been adopted. To obtain these data, a research was carried out using the SCOPUS and Web of Science databases, using the following keywords in the search: ("senior*" OR "older people" OR "elder*") AND ("interactive television" OR "itv" OR "interactive tv" OR "tv" OR "television") AND ("remote control*" OR "remote*" OR "control*" OR "tv remote*" OR "tv remote control"). Regarding the inclusion criteria, all articles addressing people with a physiological, social or psychological decline were included [15, 16]. All articles that do not address interaction, remote control or television projects aimed at older adults were excluded. Regarding the study selection and data extraction, the results were obtained initially by a detailed review of the titles and abstracts of the various articles, with a final selection being made after reading the body of the text of each article. All documents that do not meet the pre-established requirements, that were not available for review or that were in duplicate were excluded.

3 Results

From this research, 1120 potentially eligible articles were found, 439 from the Web of Science and 681 from SCOPUS databases. After a refinement by date range, subject area and keywords using the existing filtering options within the databases, it was possible to obtain 98 results (28 results from Web of Science and 60 results from SCOPUS). After removing duplicates (13 articles were removed, i.e., n = 13), results that do not address interaction, remote control, television projects oriented to older adults or that are not available for review (n = 66), 19 articles were obtained. At the end of the refinement process, articles that do not address limitations in the use of remote control by older adults or by other people with similar limitations (n = 11) were also excluded, obtaining 8 articles that satisfy the requirements for this research, i.e., that address the structure of a remote control, its functions and operations, limitations in use and possible solutions. The refinement process carried out for this research is illustrated in Fig. 1.

4 General Findings

The results found in the 8 selected articles, which address the use of remote control by older adults or other people with similar limitations, were organized in a table[1] by reference entrance with author and article names, and by topics like the characterization of the TV remote control interface, functions and operations where the remote control is used, main issues in using the remote control and solutions adopted to help using the remote control.

---

[1] To consult the table with all the obtained data about the use of TV remote control by older adults or other people with similar limitations, please access the URL: https://zenodo.org/record/428 4658.

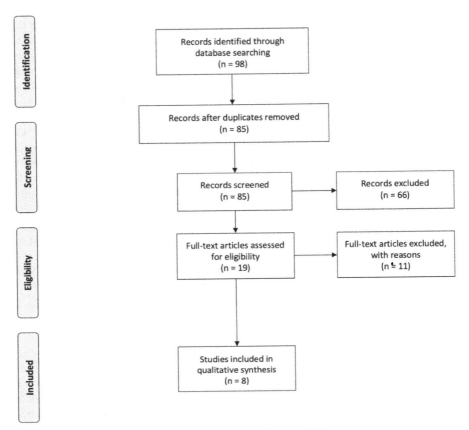

Fig. 1. PRISMA flow diagram [14].

In the subsections below, it is possible to see the main findings found in the review of the selected articles, as well as, having an insight about the older adults that participated in the studies present in the selected articles.

4.1 Participants

Before addressing the findings related to the remote control, it is relevant to mention the older adults who were invited to participate in the studies present in the reviewed articles. In this context, it is possible to see in Table 1 the number of participants that participated on the studies, as well as their age and gender.

Table 1. Details about the participants in the studies of the selected articles.

Reference	Number of participants	Age	Gender
[17]	5	Over 55	2 men 3 women
[13]	27	Mean 79.2	n/a
[18]	15	60–75 and mean age of 65	8 men 7 women
[9]	n/a	n/a	n/a
[5]	15	76–99 and mean age of 86	4 men 11 women
[7]	5	62–77 and mean age of 69.6	2 men 3 women
[19]	22	62–80	9 men 13 women
[8]	31	Mean age of 69.22	n/a

From the table it is possible to understand that the number of invited participants ranges between 5 and 31, being more frequent the existence of studies with 5 and 15 participants. The authors from the study [17] justify the conducting of their study with only 5 participants based on the theory that it is possible to obtain good results in finding usability problems with no more than five users [20]. Regarding the age, the participants are between 55 and 99 years old, with the participation of people between the ages of 60 and 70 being more frequent. Finally, it is possible to observe the gender distribution between the studies, with a good balance between the number of men and women in each study. Although, is noteworthy to mention that there is an exception in the studies [5] and [19], that features significantly more women than men invited to the respective studies. Regarding article [9], it does not present data about the participants of their study. This is due to the adoption of a system to emulate a real environment, having a fictitious character and that performs actions according to patterns learned from extensive testing together with older adults in previous studies.

4.2   Remote Control

In order to understand the use of remote control by older adults, one must first understand the type of remote control that is used to operate the television. Of the 8 selected articles, it was possible to identify TV remote controls with different interfaces, being found among the selection of articles the replacement of the remote control by another technological solution in 2 articles (Fig. 2). The first alternative was an assistive technology worn by the user that allowed the replacement of the "clicks" of the remote control by a more natural interaction (e.g., hand gestures or head movements) [17]. The other alternative to the TV remote control was a cube-shaped remote control, which also intended to use a more natural type of interaction to change channels when the cube was rotated [5].

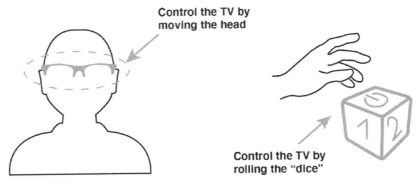

Fig. 2. Examples of alternatives to TV remote control.

In the remaining articles, TV remote controls with different interfaces were identified, highlighting: 20 traditional remote controls, which are made of the numeric keypad and set of functional/dedicated keys (e.g., specific function keys such as "source", "menu", "guide", and the four traditional directional keys combined with the "ok" and "back" button) [7, 8, 13]; 3 simplified remote controls, which may have some functional keys, directional keys, the "ok" button and the back button, but do not present a numeric keypad [7, 18, 19]; and 2 virtual remote controls, which consist in a mobile app running in a smartphone or tablet, allowing to adapt the remote control layout according to the users' needs [7, 9].

Of the physical remote controls found in the selected articles, the authors of [7] emphasize that simplified remote controls are more popular than traditional remote controls (see Fig. 3, which demonstrates the structure of a traditional remote control TV, as well as an example of a simplified remote control), so in the smart TV product market, companies such as Apple, Samsung, Huawei, Xiaomi and Baidu have increasingly invested in this type of remote controls. The same authors also point out that the remote controls developed by these companies, such as the Huawei Honor TV remote control, the Xiaomi Mi remote control, and the Samsung Smart Remote, show great similarities with the Apple TV remote, making it possible to categorize all these handhelds as simplified TV remote controls. Regarding the navigation that can be done on the Apple TV remote, it can be used the directional Keys, the "OK" button and the MENU (i.e., back) buttons. However, the version addressed by the authors of [7] was the Apple Remote made of aluminum [21], which came with the Apple TV of the 2nd or 3rd generation. The generation that is currently available in 2021 is the Apple TV of the 4th generation, called Siri Remote or Apple TV Remote [22]. This new version replaces the directional keys and the "OK" button with a Touch surface that, according to Apple [22], is used "To move around the screen, swipe up, down, left, or right. To select an item, highlight it, then press to click the Touch surface. To scroll through lists, quickly swipe up or down multiple times. If an index is next to the list, swipe right, then highlight a letter to go to that place in the list". This remote control continues to have the MENU button, serving to return to the previous screen when pressing one time, while if its pressed and hold it will go to the Home screen. It is noteworthy that in this new version the volume buttons have also been added, as well as a Play/Pause button to control the timeline of the videos, a button to view recently used apps on Apple TV or to return to the Home screen and a button called "Siri", that when is pressed on it is possible to have access to a voice virtual assistant where it can carry out voice commands.

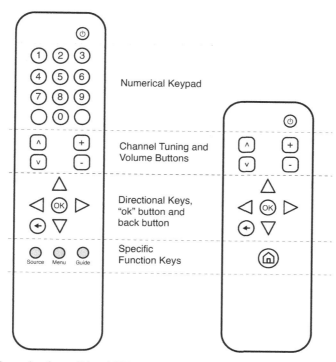

Fig. 3. Example of a traditional TV remote control and example of a simplified version.

The traditional remote control, as well as the simplified one, consists of buttons of different shapes and arranged in different ways, so it is possible to have two or more remote controls with completely different layouts. In [8] the authors define several common user interfaces for the TV remote control, using the MIL-HDBK759 model as a reference, which is a device that presents the common measures and shapes of the remote control buttons for television. In this model, the diameter of the button with the minimum fingertip area is 10 to 13 mm, while the maximum diameter of the fingertip area can reach 19 mm. Regarding the interval between single-finger continuous operations, it was 6 mm. Due to the different button shapes in the user interfaces proposed by these authors, it was not possible to identify the measures of the horizontal spacing of the numbered buttons. However, vertical spacing was defined, which was 6 mm.

4.3 Functions and Operation

This section aims to understand to what the TV remote control is used for and how it is operated. From the 8 selected articles, it stands out that the most performed operations were changing the channel or volume (5 articles mentioned this, i.e., n = 5) and without resorting to the numeric keypad (n = 5). The second most common operation with the remote control was start by pressing the power button (n = 3) and use the numeric keypad to change channels (n = 3).

The least performed operation with the remote control was press the "ok" button after finishing an operation such as changing the TV channel/volume (n = 2).

From the selected articles and as an example, it was possible to observe that the authors from [8] disclosed, in their study with TV control remotes, their operation process, being that: The first operation the participant did was tap the red Power button to turn on the TV; then use the number buttons to switch to a specific channel, which appears in the form of digits on the television screen; and at the end tap on OK button to confirm the operation.

Regarding the main function performed on television by older adults, all articles address operations that translate into watching live television. However, the different authors also addressed functions that can be performed by older adults on smart TVs, such as content search, screen mirroring, accessing video libraries and accessing applications or games (n = 4). Although not found in the articles selected for this review, the TV remote control also has the function of mute the sound transmitted by the television. Historically, this function was what led to the mass production of the first wireless TV remote by the company Zenith [23], being a function that persisted until today's TV remote controls.

4.4   Problems

After analysing the TV remote controls and what operations or functions can be performed by older adults on these devices, the conditions are provided to understand the typical problems in the use of the remote control. However, the problems do not only emerge in the TV remote control structure itself. It is also important to consider that older adults have specific characteristics that emerge with aging, such as a decrease in their physical (6 articles were found, i.e., n = 6) and cognitive (n = 4) capabilities. Thus, although in everyday life the TV remote control is a device used without great difficulty by ordinary people, older adults may have difficulties using this device.

Table 2 describes the main problems found in the review of the selected articles.

Table 2. Physical and cognitive problems of the older adult in the use of the remote control, as well as problems from the structure of the device itself.

	Problems
Older adult	Tremble hands
	Grasping issues
	Finger imprecision
	Visual impairments
	Memory decrease
	Learnability decrease

(continued)

Table 2. (*continued*)

	Problems
Remote control	Large number of functions
	Unfamiliar functions
	Small labels
	Small symbols
	Small buttons
	Small gap between buttons
	Inflexible layout (buttons cannot be reorganized)
	Small device
	Lack of backlight
	Requires stiff posture to avoid losing infrared signal

From the 8 selected articles, users might face: memory problems and need more time to learn [7, 13]; tremble hands, grasping issues, fingers imprecision and visual impairments to see small content [5, 8, 9]. In this context, these users have difficulty using remote controls that have: too many functions or have an unfamiliar layout of the buttons (n = 2); small labels, symbols and buttons, and little or no gap at all between them (n = 5). It is noteworthy to add that the difficulty increases when using a TV remote control with small buttons while standing [8] and that small buttons can lead to a miss click [7]; Older adults can use directional buttons to operate like a mouse/keyboard on a smart TV (n = 3), although physical keypads of the traditional TV Remote Controls are also uncomfortable, since it requires intense concentration [7]; They do not properly present information to understand how to use it (e.g. simplified remote control), just as it is ineffective to use on-screen instructions, since older adults frequently ignore it [7]. Other identified issues related to the remote control are that the layout cannot be changed based on personal preference, it is easy to get lost, does not have a backlight and requires a stiff posture to avoid losing the infrared signal [7]. Alternatives to the conventional use of a TV remote control have also been identified in the articles. In the study of the authors [18], Xiaomi® smart TV was used to run an Android operating system, and the virtual voice assistant integrated in the system was used. From this system, it is possible to use the TV remote control to perform voice commands. However, some impairments were found in this virtual voice assistant, such as lack of recognition of certain languages and low accuracy of the speech recognition, mainly user accent and when there is environmental noise. Ouyang and Zhou [7] also point out, in addition to the limited accuracy of speech recognition, the difficulty in processing vocabulary in professional fields and for managing grammatical problems in oral conversation. These authors suggest another alternative, such as a touchscreen. This latest solution makes it possible to use apps and thus provide a more flexible TV remote control interface. However, the authors of [7] point out some limitations, such as the lack of haptic feedback, leading to the need for greater attention shift between the TV remote control and the television. The same applies to the Apple TV of the 4th generation, which features a touchpad or touch surface that, according to the publication in [24], served to emulate the touchscreens of iPhone and iPads. In the same publication, more problems inherent to the Apple device are highlighted, such as: the difficulty in finding the touchpad due to the device appearing all in the same colour: and both the device and the touchpad itself, are too small, making it difficult to input gestures.

4.5 Solutions

Of the 8 selected articles, one of the solutions that stood out was to make the TV remote control interface simpler and clearer (4 articles mentioned this, i.e., n = 4), removing the numeric buttons (including some dedicated function keys) and navigating with the back and forward buttons (n = 3). Ouyang and Zhou [7] points out that simplified Remote controls are more popular than traditional ones, so remote controls like the one associated to the Apple TV, regardless of the generation addressed in this study, are designed to eliminate problems caused by too many buttons on traditional counterpart. [13] corroborates this statement saying that a simplified interface allows for a better intuitive operation behavior. However, [7] points out that there are also problems that must be considered when using simplified remote controls. Although these appear to be larger and easier to use, older adults highlighted that these handsets present too little information to understand how to operate the remote control correctly, thus requiring a balance in the amount of information to be displayed. Other solutions found to simplify the remote control were the use of an application with a navigation menu on the TV screen and resort to application's mirroring [17]. However, [7] point to possible problems from these last two solutions. Despite the increase of their popularity among older adults, as well as their portability and flexibility of the layout, when using the touchscreen for mirroring or when using navigation menus on the TV screen controlled by more simplified remote controls (such as the Apple TV remote), they require more attention shift between the tv remote control and television from the user due to lack of haptic feedback. Another solution that was found in the selected articles was the redesign of the shape of the buttons (n = 4), despite the fact that [8] states that there are mixed viewpoints, some saying the button shape has little impact on operation speed, others saying that the contact area of the finger during operation varies with the button shape. Nevertheless, one of the solutions is to increase the size of the buttons [9, 19]. If it is not possible to increase the size of the buttons, a square-shaped button will be easier to press [8]. However, in the same study, it is highlighted that the number buttons of the TV remote controls have mostly rectangular or rounded shapes, which users are familiar with on both interfaces. Another point to consider is that press buttons should be set up independently [13] and be distinguishable [8], with enough gap between the buttons to not cause confusion to the user. Buttons should also be grouped according to their functions [7, 8], allowing for faster use of the required keys. The authors from [8] adds that the arrangement of the button blocks should also be done accordingly to what older adults are already used to. It was also proposed as a solution a way to help the user to understand the remote control interface (n = 3), despite due to past experience, older adults are used to pressing buttons without texts or indicator symbols [13]. Enhanced colours, higher contrast of the colours and assistive messages (if written, readable fonts should be used) are some of the solutions for visual and audible feedback/cues [17, 19], as well as adding visual drawings that support the textual description [19]. Regarding the remote control itself, it should fit perfectly in the palm of the hand and be possible to be used with only one hand [5, 19]. If none of the previous solutions meets the user's needs, alternatives to remote control have also been identified. For example, the click on a button can be replaced by different input modalities (n = 5), such as voice commands (n = 4), Gestures (n = 3; the authors from [9] proposed to use the gesture defined as swabbing - pressing the finger against the screen at one point and moving the finger towards the place the user really wants to tap on, and then raising the finger), eye-free interactive technologies [7], gaze and the use of gyroscopes and accelerometers [19]. Another option is to replace the remote control with a touch screen device, making it possible to adapt the remote control layout according to the user's needs [7, 8]; or use a cube to replace the "click" with the natural movement of this object, whose face at the top will play a role on the TV-set [5].

Table 3 lists the main findings regarding the solutions found for problems in the use of the TV remote control.

Table 3. Solutions found for problems in the use of the TV remote control.

Solutions	Description
Simplify the layout	Remove numeric keypad Remove some specific function keys Insert a simple navigation menu on the TV screen Replace click of button by natural interaction (e.g., voice commands)
Mirror applications	Use touchscreen devices for specific functions
Redesign shape of the buttons	Bigger size Square-shaped Separated from each other Distinguishable
Organize the buttons	Acceptable gap distance from each other Order by functions Organize with familiar layout
Insert visual and audible cues	Enhanced colours Higher colour contrast Assistive messages Visual drawings with text description
Needs to be physically comfortable	Fit in the palm of the hand Usable with only one hand
Alternatives to the TV remote control	Replace by a touch screen device Replace by a dice shaped cube

5 Discussion and Summary of Main Results

This systematic review was carried out to understand the studies that have been developed in the last 5 years regarding the use of TV remote controls by older adults, considering the difficulties they have at the physical and cognitive level in using this device. In this review it was also possible to identify a set of solutions proposed by the different authors to overcome the identified problems when older adults use the TV remote control. It was also possible to understand, in the first analysis, the participants who were invited to the studies carried out in the selected articles, highlighting the organization of groups of 5 or 15 participants and aged between 60 and 70 years. Regarding the gender, the numbers are balanced, although more women than men participate in these studies. Subsequently, an analysis was made to understand how the interface of a remote control can be structured, which can be composed of a set of functional keys and present (or not) a numeric keypad. As an option, the remote control can be replaced by a touchscreen device (such as a smartphone), allowing greater flexibility of the remote-control layout. Another suggestion is to use assistive technologies for natural interactions, replacing the "clicks" on the remote control by more than one type of input modalities, such as voice commands, gestures or gaze. It can also be replaced by objects such as a cube, whose movement of the object through rotation allows a function to be triggered. Regarding the usefulness of the remote control, it is used in particular to switch channels and changing the volume of the TV-set, preferably using functional keys when compared to the numeric keypad. When the remote control is used to explore the contents of the Smart TVs, the functional keys are also used.

After understanding how the remote control is organized and realizing what it is used for, the conditions are given to understand the main requirements suggested in the different articles selected for this review. First of all, older adults have difficulties in understanding interfaces that have too many contents or functions, so the interface of the remote control should be simplified, removing for example the numeric keypad, in order to make it easier to find the desired buttons and use the TV remote control more quickly. If it is chosen to simplify the TV remote control interface, it should be considered as well that these users often ignore on-screen instructions, so it should be inserted navigation menus on the TV screen that is simple to understand and easy to use.

Although users, such as older adults, are used to using remote controls without text or indicator symbols, it is suggested that the button on a remote control has visual, tactile or audible feedback/cues, in order to understand whether the button was successfully pressed, or to have information to understand the purpose of the respective button. Regarding the shape of the buttons, older adults have difficulties using buttons that are too small, so it should be considered to create remote controls with large buttons and preferably square-shaped buttons, since this is the shape that brings a minor chance of error by performing a miss click. It must also be considered that buttons that are too close together, make the target audience of this study to have difficulties in pressing the right button. This is due to their tremble hands and lack of dexterity, requiring the remote control to have adequate distance between buttons. Also, one should consider the adaptability of these users, who may have difficulties in handling interfaces that are unfamiliar to them, so buttons that have the same or similar functions must be grouped according to what the users are already used to. Regarding more complex operations on television, the remote control is not a good option for these users to be used as if it were a mouse or computer keyboard, requiring too much concentration in addition to being uncomfortable. It should always be chosen solutions that do not require the use of two hands on the remote control, as well as devices that fit in the user's palm. Lastly, the TV remote control usually has physical buttons and does not have the flexibility to reorganize its layout according to the user's needs. Other problems detected are: due to its small size is easy to lose the device; it has no backlight on the buttons; and requires the user to make a stiff position while holding the remote control, to avoid losing the infrared signal. A possible solution is to use devices such as the smartphone, which has a touch screen that allows to remodel the layout according to the user's preferences, and that has features that allows to find the device and can connect it via Bluetooth instead of using the infrared signal. However, touchscreen devices do not have physical buttons, which requires more attention-switching from the user. Another alternative is to use different modalities inputs, such as voice commands instead of "clicking" on the remote control. But this alternative also has its own limitations, for example, low recognition accuracy. However, according to the various authors of the selected articles, this latest solution provides a simple to use voice search (such as search for a specific tv service content by saying the name of the television program), as well as resulting in the best user experience for older people.

6 Conclusion

In view of the review that was carried out, it was possible to understand the use of remote control by older adults, as well as to understand how the TV remote control interface is composed and what operations or functions are most used. Regarding the use of the remote control, it was possible to verify that the main difficulties in its use come from both physical and cognitive problems of the user, as well as the interface of the remote controls not being properly designed for this population, being possible to conclude that these devices have room for improvement to facilitate their use. In this context, the solutions proposed by the different authors were observed, which are mainly based on the simplification of the TV remote control interface and the redesign of its buttons. Regarding the interface based on the remote control, it was possible to verify that it can be composed by a set of functional keys and present (or not) a numeric keypad. It has also been demonstrated that there are alternatives to the remote control, such as a touchscreen device (the smartphone, for example), allowing greater flexibility of a new TV remote control layout according to the user needs. Other alternatives are the replacement of the "clicking" of the buttons by other input modalities, such as voice commands or gestures. However, these solutions also feature their own limitations. Regardless of the conclusion obtained, it should be considered that this study is limited to the interpretation made to the data obtained from the selected databases, as well as the data in this review are limited between the years 2016 and 2020.

References

1. Reis, L., Caravau, H., Silva, T., Almeida, P.: Automatic creation of TV content to integrate in seniors viewing activities. In: Abásolo, M.J., Almeida, P., Pina Amargós, J. (eds.) jAUTI 2016. CCIS, vol. 689, pp. 32–46. Springer, Cham (2017). ISBN: 978-3-319-63321-3. https://doi.org/10.1007/978-3-319-63321-3_3

2. Carvalho, D., Silva, T., Abreu, J.: Interaction models for iTV services for elderly people. In: Abásolo, M.J., Silva, T., González, N.D. (eds.) jAUTI 2018. CCIS, vol. 1004, pp. 89–98. Springer, Cham (2019). https://doi.org/10.1007/978-3-030-23862-9_7

3. Silva, T., Abreu, J., Antunes, M., Almeida, P., Silva, V., Santinha, G.: +TV4E: interactive television as a support to push information about social services to the elderly. Procedia Comput. Sci. **100**, 580–585 (2016). https://doi.org/10.1016/j.procs.2016.09.198

4. Abreu, J.F., Almeida, P., Silva, T.: iNeighbour TV: a social TV application to promote wellness of senior citizens. In: Information Systems and Technologies for Enhancing Health and Social Care, vol. 221, p. 19 (2013). https://doi.org/10.4018/978-1-4666-3667-5.ch001

5. Oliveira, A.P., Vairinhos, M., Mealha, Ó.: Proposal of a tangible interface to enhance seniors' TV experience: UX evaluation of SIX. In: Abásolo, M.J., Abreu, J., Almeida, P., Silva, T. (eds.) jAUTI 2017. CCIS, vol. 813, pp. 135–149. Springer, Cham (2018). ISBN: 978-3-319-90170-1. https://doi.org/10.1007/978-3-319-90170-1_10

6. Cardoso, R., Rodrigues, A., Coelho, M., Tavares, T., Oliveira, R., Silva, T.: IOM4TV: an AT-based solution for people with motor disabilities supported in iTV. In: Abásolo, M.J., Silva, T., González, N.D. (eds.) jAUTI 2018. CCIS, vol. 1004, pp. 99–114. Springer, Cham (2019). https://doi.org/10.1007/978-3-030-23862-9_8

7. Ouyang, X., Zhou, J.: How to help older adults move the focus on a smart TV? Exploring the effects of arrow hints and element size consistency. Int. J. Hum. Comput. Interact. **35**, 1420–1436 (2019). https://doi.org/10.1080/10447318.2018.1534346

8. Zhao, R.-Q., Chen, L.-H.: Research on interface design for the elderly. In: Stephanidis, C., Antona, M. (eds.) HCII 2020. CCIS, vol. 1226, pp. 128–135. Springer, Cham (2020). https://doi.org/10.1007/978-3-030-50732-9_18

9. Gomez-Sanz, J.J., Campillo Sanchez, P.: Domain independent regulative norms for evaluating performance of assistive solutions. Pervasive Mob. Comput. **34**, 79–90 (2017). https://doi.org/10.1016/j.pmcj.2016.08.006

10. Parada, R., Nur, K., Melia-Segui, J., Pous, R.: Smart surface: RFID-based gesture recognition using k-means algorithm. In: 12th International Conference on Intelligent Environments - IE 2016, pp. 111–118 (2016). https://doi.org/10.1109/IE.2016.25

11. Kumar, K.S.C.: Stereo-vision based smart TV control. In: 2015 IEEE International Conference on Computer Graphics, Vision and Information Security, CGVIS 2015, pp. 67–71. Institute of Electrical and Electronics Engineers Inc. (2016). https://doi.org/10.1109/CGVIS.2015.7449895

12. Pereira, L.: Princípios orientadores de design de interfaces para aplicações ITV orientadas para seniores portugueses (2013). https://hdl.handle.net/10216/70261

13. Cheng, Y.-W., Chen, L.-H., Liu, Y.-C.: Intuitive interface design for elderly-demented users. In: Meen, T.-H., Prior, S.D., L.A.D.K.-T. (eds.) Applied System Innovation - Proceedings of the International Conference on Applied System Innovation, ICASI 2015, pp. 675–679. CRC Press/Balkema (2016). https://www.researchgate.net/publication/303885107_Intuitive_interface_design_for_elderly-demented_users

14. Liberati, A., et al.: The PRISMA statement for reporting systematic reviews and meta-analyses of studies that evaluate health care interventions: explanation and elaboration (2009). https://doi.org/10.1371/journal.pmed.1000100

15. Paúl, C.: Envelhecimento ativo e redes de suporte social. Sociologia **15**, 275–287 (2005). http://ler.letras.up.pt/uploads/ficheiros/3732.pdf

16. Ferreira, S.: Tecnologias de informação e comunicação e o cidadão sénior: estudo sobre o impacto em variáveis psicossociais e a conceptualização de serviços com e para o cidadão sénior. Tese de doutoramento (2013). http://ria.ua.pt/handle/10773/12336

17. Cardoso, R., Rodrigues, A., Costa, V., Silva, T., Oliveira, R., Tavares, T.: Improving a software framework from an assistive technology application for iTV. In: Abásolo, M.J., Kulesza, R., Pina, J.D., Amargós, (eds.) jAUTI 2019. CCIS, vol. 1202, pp. 31–49. Springer, Cham (2019). https://doi.org/10.1007/978-3-030-56574-9_3

18. Dou, J., Qin, J., Wang, Q., Zhao, Q.: Identification of usability problems and requirements of elderly Chinese users for smart TV interactions. Behav. Inf. Technol. **38**, 664–677 (2019). https://doi.org/10.1080/0144929X.2018.1551423

19. Lopez, J.P., Moreno, F., Popa, M., Hernandez-Penaloza, G., Alvarez, F.: Data analysis from cognitive games interaction in Smart TV applications for patients with Parkinson's, Alzheimer's, and other types of dementia. AI EDAM Artif. Intell. Eng. Des. Anal. Manuf. **33**, 442–457 (2019). https://doi.org/10.1017/S0890060419000386

20. Nielsen, J., Landauer, T.K.: Mathematical model of the finding of usability problems. In: Proceedings of the Conference on Human Factors in Computing Systems (1993). https://doi.org/10.1145/169059.169166

21. Apple: Use your Apple Remote with your Apple TV. https://support.apple.com/en-us/HT200131

22. Apple: Use your Siri Remote or Apple TV Remote with your Apple TV. https://support.apple.com/en-us/HT205305

23. Luplow, W.C., Taylor, J.I.: Channel surfing redux: a brief history of the TV remote control and a tribute to its coinventors. IEEE Consum. Electron. Mag. (2012). https://doi.org/10.1109/MCE.2012.2207149

24. Gartenberg, C.: The Apple TV's touchpad swipes and misses at being a good remote. https://www.theverge.com/2021/2/25/22300891/apple-tv-siri-remote-touchpad-button-design-form-function

IDTV Application to Promote the Gait of the Elderly

Magdalena Rosado[1](✉) ⓘ, María J. Abásolo[2,3](✉) ⓘ, and Telmo Silva[4] ⓘ

[1] Faculty of Medical Sciences, Catholic University of Santiago de Guayaquil, Guayaquil, Ecuador
`maria.rosadoa@info.unlp.edu.ar`
[2] Faculty of Computer Sciences, National University of La Plata (UNLP), La Plata, Argentina
`mjabasolo@lidi.info.unlp.edu.ar`
[3] CICPBA Scientific Research Commission of the Buenos Aires Province, La Plata, Argentina
[4] University of Aveiro, Aveiro, Portugal
`tsilva@ua.pt`

Abstract. The introduction of technology in daily life activities has facilitated routines, some of them related to the quality of life of elderly, who are commonly considered as an independent population. The present project aims to develop an interactive application for television with content related to exercises to enhance gait function of elderly. This paper addresses the evaluation of the functional condition through a set of tests, the development of localized exercise routines, the architecture of the interactive application and the planned evaluation.

Keywords: Independent elderly · Gait test · Platform · Interactive exercises · Television

1 Introduction

The considerable increase of the number of elderly adults brings a proportional increase in chronic degenerative diseases [15]. Nowadays, due to the increase of life expectancy, societies are facing an increase in the number of elderly adults [22]. In this perspective, challenges must be overcome due to new health demands, resulting in greater and longer use of primary care services [24]. Physiological changes derived from aging can cause falls, which are one of the main risks of generating disability in elderly persons [33], i.e., compromising independence and autonomy. Persons over 65 years of age may present difficulties in walking, which may cause accidents. These accidents can cause serious effects, affecting old persons' physical condition. The following is a review of studies with digital tools to improve physical ability of the elderly.

The research of several authors shows that technology has been introduced to improve daily life activities of older adults. In [28] a review of Information and Communication Technology oriented to the active aging of old persons with the aim of improving their self-care and empowerment of health care is presented. The results showed that mobile applications and web applications were the most used. Nevertheless, there is also a

© Springer Nature Switzerland AG 2021
M. J. Abásolo et al. (Eds.): jAUTI 2020, CCIS 1433, pp. 134–146, 2021.
https://doi.org/10.1007/978-3-030-81996-5_10

prevalence of the use of specific sensors to monitor or control the elderly; and in relation to interactive television, some solutions were found that allow elderly people to easily set reminders for their medical care, and entertainment programs to have mental and social well-being. [9] presented a systematic review of 39 articles on the use of new technologies to evaluate physical activity and its relationship with health. The results indicated that daytime and night-time physical activity can be recorded with smart electronic devices with motion sensors allowing active and passive monitoring, providing the possibility of remote and longitudinal evaluation of physical activity. In [6] a systematic search of mobile health technologies is presented; the results identified that from several mobile technologies that are used to monitor elderly adults, 69.5% include data visualization and only 36% include self-reporting.

The aging process brings impacts on various aspects of people's lives, including social, economical, and health. Basically, elderly tend to spend most of their time at home and watching television. It is undoubtedly the preferred entertainment option to enjoy free time; therefore, this activity has become a social, cultural and political phenomenon of great impact [28].

In [29] we present a work related to the field of physiotherapy and it consists in designing an interactive TV application allowing the construction of care models of the elderly incorporating remote exercise plans, similar to those executed in real time. In the present article we extend the aforementioned article, and the rest of the article is organized as follows: Sect. 2 shows related work with the use of television, and with the physical activity of the elderly; Sect. 3 shows considerations around assessment of the functional gait condition and the design of exercise plan oriented to reduce gait alterations; Sect. 4 explains the services of the application; Sect. 5 describes the evaluation planning; and finally, Sect. 6 states synthesis and future work.

2 Related Work

2.1 The Elderly and Television

Television consumption in elderly people is one of the primary activities [5]. Although television is an economical and convenient medium for the elderly, it is used as a means of information, entertainment, companionship and contact with the world [13].

In the first place, there tends to be a need on the part of the elderly to be constantly informed. For example, [19] expresses that people over 65 years of age have a special interest in the events that occur on the planet because they reach the last stage of psychosocial development and seek a "fusion with the world", being television one of their main tools to stay informed. [10] describes television as a window to the world. This means of communication becomes a daily companion keeping elderly abreast of events or facts that occur in the world, [12], indicating that this search for information is expressed in different ways. Some become addicted to the point of watching programs all day long, others are more selective and only choose to watch local news. There are also those who have the need to listen to someone, and then express themselves according to their feelings and discernment.

The second reason why the elderly watch television is for entertainment. They like to recreate themselves with television content so as to have elements of conversations with people around them. [31] in a study conducted by asking the elderly what they miss most about television programs. He found that the elderly respondents missed entertainment topics more than informational content.

The result of this information is that news and entertainment programs are the most popular for them. Both cases are narrative facts, which clearly establishes that subjects of these ages do not like to be alone.

And the third reason is that television acts as a companion [30], considered as a point of union between the elderly and the outside world. Thus, there are also people of such ages who live alone, so it is established that television is a compensatory and permeable instrument -of acceptance- for them, which makes their moments of loneliness bearable.

In view of the above, a clear vision of how people over 65 years of age use television in their daily life is presented, resorting to it as a substitute for company. In fact, according to the research, it can be established that the small screen provides people of these ages with programs or conduits of social interrelation that make loneliness dissipate quickly, according to research results. It is still being discussed if the television is a window that invites to know the world or if it can become the transporter of the subject.

2.2 Physical Activities of the Elderly

Physical activity decreases progressively with age [8]. As a result of inactivity, elderly people experience loss of independence (and increased lack of strength, flexibility or endurance to rise from a chair, walk or dress independently) [25]. There are also other problems associated with lack of exercise like: cerebrovascular disease, high blood pressure, colon and breast cancer, diabetes type 2, metabolic syndrome, obesity, osteoporosis, sarcopenia, cognitive decline, anxiety and depression [3].

In order to aspire to a good quality of life in old age, it is important to achieve a healthy and active physical and psychological life, facing life events in a positive and constructive way, developing a capacity to control external events so that they bring benefits [22].

The elderly must maintain physical activity, while interacting with other people their age, who provide social support; all of which together with a meaning of their life through spirituality, religious or not, that will allow them an optimal quality of life. The social representation of the elderly commonly expresses the idea of social isolation, cognitive impairment, lack of physical activity and inability to contribute economically to society and family [1]. Several authors highlight the importance of social involvement of the elderly, as well as the need to modify negative stereotypes around old age, and the importance also of participation of the elderly in community programs [11, 12].

The World Health Organization highlights the important role of physical activity in achieving healthy aging and quality of life [23].

Although the positive effects of exercise on the well-being and independent life of elderly adults are well known, many seniors lack the access to exercise facilities, or the skills and motivation to exercise at home [16]. Thus, environments that promote physical activity should be promoted.

3 Study Considerations

3.1 Assessment of the Functional Gait Condition of the Elderly

One of the best ways to assess the health status of the elderly is through functional assessment, which provides objective data that can indicate future health conditions [7].

In order to perform functional assessments, it is necessary to apply tests. Following it is listed a set of possible ones': Katz Index, Barthel Index, Lawton and Brody Scale, Tinetti scale, Walking endurance test and "timed get up and go". These tests are easy to apply and are duly validated [2]. When quantifying the functional condition of an elderly person's gait, a set of difficulties arise, since most of the tests proposed in the literature have been developed for the young or adult population and are difficult, inappropriate and unsafe for the elderly [34].

For this research study, the following tests will be used to identify and know the state of the person, its level of independence and its cognitive capacity and the functional condition of the gait.

1) Independent Test [14]:

- Barthel Index: it assesses a person's ability to independently perform 10 basic activities of daily living such as eat, move from chair to bed and back, perform personal hygiene, go to the toilet, bathe, move around, go up and down stairs, dress, and maintain bowel and urinary control.
- Lawton and Brody Scale: it assesses functional capacity using eight items: ability to use the telephone, shop, prepare food, take care of the house, wash clothes, use means of transportation, and responsibility for medication and administration of their finances.

2) Cognitive Test:

- The Lobo Cognitive Mini-Test assesses a wide range of cognitive aspects, with a well-organized structure and well-defined components [20]. It is a test with questions that are gathered in five groups to assess spatio-temporal orientation, immediate memory fixation, concentration and calculation capacity, language and spatial construction. These results will make it possible to check if indeed older people, in relation to younger people, present a lower competence in all cognitive tasks, if they use the same strategies for problem solving, among others [21].

3) Gait Tests:

- Tinetti scale has two domains: gait and balance; its main objective is to detect risk of falling, its predictive value is greater than the value in the muscle test; it is composed of nine balance items and seven gait items [31, 32].
- Test "timed get up and go", is a test designed to quantify mobility, and functional capacity of elderly patients, and that correlates with the result of other tests that evaluate balance and gait, being a reliable and valid test for the quantification of functional

mobility, standing out from this with respect to others for its easy performance, and that does not require expert personnel to evaluate it; that can also be useful in the monitoring of clinical changes over time [26].

With the results of these four tests, it is possible to obtain more objective information on the physical and cognitive function of the person, which translates into the ability to perform, independently, the activities of daily living. These tests will also allow the assessment of the risk of falling, allowing to determine if there are alterations in gait that require intervention, and allowing to assess the presence of possible neurological or musculoskeletal disorders.

For the use of the tests, functional category scales will be identified, which correspond to a series of categories in which a judgment validated by health experts must be issued, indicating the degree to which a characteristic is present in the reference tests. The scale requires a qualitative assessment of certain aspects of an activity and according to the category scale, and can be:

- Numerical (e.g. from 1 to 5);
- Estimated (a lot, a little, not at all; always - usually - sometimes - never; etc.);
- Descriptive (a description of the characteristic possessed or the description that best reflects the situation selected).

3.2   Development of Exercise Plans for the Elderly to Reduce Gait Alterations

To build an exercise program, certain parameters mentioned by [17, 27] should be followed:

a) Type/Mode of Activity: it details the activity to be executed/carried out? with the muscle groups involved and that maintain continuous contractions (for a given period), the exercises can be anaerobic or aerobic;
b) Duration: variations in exercise time in a continuous or intermittent manner, depending on the organization of each session and can range from minutes to hours;
c) Frequency: number of days per week to exercise, depending on the availability and training level of the participant;
d) Progression: by gradual ascent in the difficulty of the exercise, influenced by the level of the participant;
e) Intensity: it reflects the speed at which the activity is performed, or the magnitude of the effort required to perform an exercise or activity, and it depends on the individual's level of exercise and physical fitness [24];
f) Training density: it is the relationship between activity and rest, considered both as intra-session density (inter-series; inter-blocks or exercises) and as inter-session density (between sessions or training units) [18].

For the exercise routine, the principle of progression will be taken into account. This refers to the gradual increase or variation that the exercises will have so that the elderly person maintains independence for longer periods of time with better functional capacity, involving fun or motivation when performing physical activity. In this scenario, the aspects considered for the ludification gamification? of the elderly persons, will allow enhancing the skills that are required in the functional condition of walking, promoting a better performance and, consequently, promoting a better quality of life.

In this scenario, the aspects considered for the ludification of the elderly, will allow enhancing the skills that are required to be rewarded in the functional condition of walking, which would allow energizing their better performance and therefore their quality of life.

The exercise routine for the functional condition of walking should include the following groups:

- Warm-up phase exercises: these are the ones that allow a previous preparation so that joints and muscles are not weakened before a movement and can result in an injury (Fig. 1).
- Walking exercises: These will allow the muscle groups to work in coordination to move the legs forward (Fig. 2).
- Relaxation exercises: Allow the muscles of the body to relax, reduce tension or stress in the muscles (Fig. 3).

For the development of the exercises of the gait functional condition, the exercise guide for frail elderly described in the book [4] will be followed.

The exercise videos will be developed by a work team from the Faculty of Medical Sciences of the Catholic University of Santiago de Guayaquil (UCSG) - Ecuador, made up of physiotherapists, students and support technicians.

a)   b)

Fig. 1. Warm-up phase exercises: a) Ankle circumduction (https://bit.ly/378NKXP); b) Hip circumduction (https://bit.ly/3qU8BFE)

a)   b)

Fig. 2. Walking exercises: a) Alternating Heel Toe (https://bit.ly/3qU8BFE); b) Unipodal Support and Ankle Circumduction (https://bit.ly/3qU8BFE)

a)   b)

Fig. 3. Relaxation exercises: a) Hip lateralization (http://bit.ly/3qU8BFE); b) Gait in the same place (http://bit.ly/3qU8BFE)

4   Application Architecture

The proposed interactive application MarchGymTV will be supported by a microservices architecture (MSA) that allows defining, publishing and using specific solutions that meet the requirements of different types of users, so that they can use the application without implementing programming changes. Each microservice is a functional unit in the technological solution and seeks to be as independent as possible from the rest. Among its application advantages it can be listed: a) modularity and scalability of the application in case more functionalities need to be added, b) easy maintenance because they are pieces of code focused on a specific requirement, and c) freedom to choose the best languages and technology to be used in the development because the communication through Application Programming Interfaces is language neutral, flexible easy to administrate and use, and c) the application will store all the corresponding information to be used by the users.

The application will store all the information corresponding to the senior's data, test results, number of times he/she accesses the videos and badges obtained.

The programming language of the software solution will be defined based on the trends of development tools that similar applications use as long as it meets the needs of the project.

The design of the interface will be user-centered, in such a way that it facilitates the interaction of the senior with the application.

4.1 Microservices Available from the Application

Figure 4 shows the microservices of the MarchGymTV application.

The requirements that the different users may have are:

a) Older adult must first register in the application and fill out an information form that will create the access credentials for the option to enter the system, then must perform the test of independence and functional condition of walking that will serve as selection criteria to perform the exercise routine, all these steps are performed only once, except for the test that at the end of the training stage should be applied later to buy performance. To perform the exercise routine the senior will have to access the application and work daily his exercise routine that will be supported by the use of videos, it has been considered to manage scores and badges that the user can acquire for each fulfillment of exercise routine that he performs. To perform the steps, the independent person will be accompanied by a physiotherapist or researcher of the study to guide him/her or help him/her understand how the application works, when he/she starts working with it.

b) System administrator will have a different work environment than the senior, since it is a type of user with certain privileges, the administrator user must register and access through a username and password that will allow him to manage and administer the options with which the client interacts and establish the requirements of the application, which are:

– User Registration (customers and administrators), from this option you can register the data of each user and provide assistance related to forgotten passwords, update profiles and user data.
– Independence, cognitive and gait functional condition evaluation test,
– Badges, you will be able to create and categorize the score badges by access time of each video that will be counted by day and week. At the end of the day it will show the total points scored per video and at the end of the week it will show the accumulated total.
– Content management (videos) will be carried out through the Plex Server application, which must be previously installed in the storage server, this will allow adding useful information to the videos that are managed from there.
– Reporting based on criteria: results by type of test, number of registered and active users by type of exercise, access by user to verify days, times and routines worked by each independent senior citizen, among others.

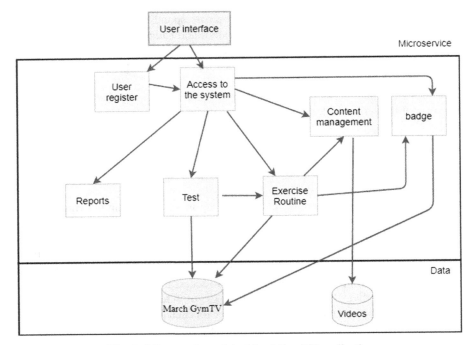

Fig. 4. Microservices of the MarchGymTV application

4.2 Process Diagram

Figure 5 shows the steps that the senior will follow using the MarchGymTV application. The steps to follow are:

1. The elderly adult must register
2. If the registration is successful, then the number of exercise days is assigned to zero so that it will subsequently count each of the days that the routine is practiced.
3. The participant performs the independent evaluation test, if the result shows that he/she is independent then he/she develops the walking test, otherwise he/she finishes, since the application is aimed only to independent seniors.
4. The participant performs the gait test, based on the result obtained, it suggests the type of exercises that he or she should perform: i) null gait exercises, ii) mild gait exercises, iii) moderate gait exercises and iv) strong gait exercises.
5. The old adult starts his/her exercises and the day counter and his/her score achievement record are updated, which will allow him/her to access badges that will motivate him/her to continue in the rehabilitation process.
6. If the number of days is less than the program duration then return to step 5, otherwise the evaluation process is performed.
7. If the evaluation process is successful the process ends, otherwise return to step 4.

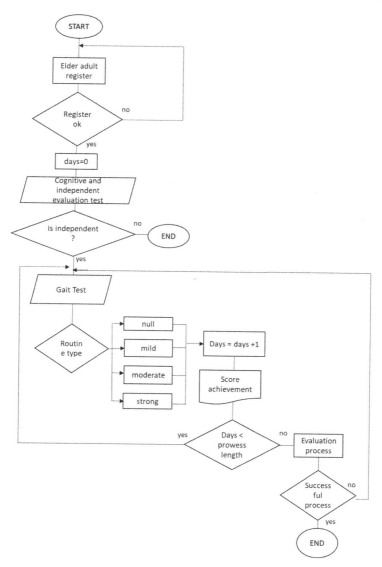

Fig. 5. Process diagram of MarchGymTV application

5 Evaluation Planning

We plan to evaluate the elderly gait performance evolution with the use of the MarchGymTV application (Fig. 6).

First, the study population to which the process detailed in the previous section will be applied to was selected; the independent old adults of the "Dr. Arsenio de la Torre Marcillo" Municipal Gerontological Center in the city of Guayaquil, Ecuador, were chosen. By resolution of the National Emergency Operations Center, the places that are with people in conditions of vulnerability or priority attention group must have a capacity control to ensure the safety of people. It is intended to test the application with 10 old adults. For this study, there are two user groups:

1. Therapists of the UCSG; and.
2. Elderly adults from the gerontological center.

In relation to the functional test, a test plan is foreseen that will allow reviewing the usability of the tool in the evaluation of the performance of the exercises that will include the response times of the system and the stability of the functionalities. As a result, an action report of the application will be created.

Experts in physical therapy indicate the importance of re-evaluating the old adult to know if he/she changed to a functional category classified as null, mild, moderate, strong or remained in the same. This will allow the research team to identify if the exercise routine used was beneficial in the prevention, development and rehabilitation of the old adult's gait.

6   Synthesis and Future Work

The present work refers to several previous studies that describe interactive TV applications that incorporate exercise routines to reduce gait disturbances. It also refers to different assessment tests that are applied to help in the evaluation of the old adult's independence, cognitive and gait.

This work proposes an exercise plan by type of functional category classified by null, mild, moderate and strong. In relation to the usage and interaction of the old adults with the application, activities with gamification will be integrated so that they obtain points for each exercise routine performed and badges as they progress.

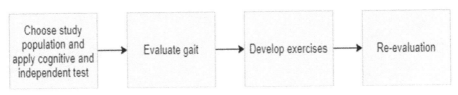

Fig. 6. MarchGymTV evaluation planning

As future work, it is expected to evaluate the application by monitoring it in the place where the exercise routines will be performed, in order to determine the levels of difficulty by type of routine and the commitment of each old adult.

Acknowledgements. This work was partially granted by Perez-Guerrero Trust Fund for South-South Cooperation, UNITED NATIONS, INT/19/K08 *"Digital Terrestrial Television Applied to the Improvement of Developing Countries Peoples: Argentina, Brazil and Cuba"*.

References

1. Aponte, V.: Calidad de vida en la tercera edad. Ajayu. Órgano de Difusión Científica del Departamento de Psicología de la Universidad Católica Boliviana San Pablo. **13**(2), 152–182 (2015). (in Spanish)
2. Baldini, M., Bernal, P.A., Jiménez, R., Garatachea, N.: Valoración de la condición física funcional en ancianos. Revista Digit. EFDeportes 103 (2006). (in Spanish)
3. Bayego, E., Subirats, G., Iñigo, S.: Prescripción de ejercicio físico: indicaciones, posología y efectos adversos. Med. Clin. **138**(1), 18–24 (2012). (in Spanish)
4. Best-Martini, E., Jones-DiGenova, K.A.: Ejercicio para ancianos frágiles. Cinética humana (2014). (in Spanish)
5. Bustos Martínez, L. Mando a distancia y soledad: vejez y consumo televisivo en hogares unipersonales en el distrito de Usera (2019). (in Spanish)
6. Cajamarca, G., Herskovic, V., Rossel, P.O.: Monitoreo de la información sobre la salud de los adultos mayores mediante tecnología móvil: una revisión sistemática de la literatura. Actas **31**(1), 62 (2019). (in Spanish)
7. Carmenaty, I., Soler, L.: Evaluación funcional del anciano. Rev. Cubana **18**(3), 184 (2002)
8. Centers for Disease Control and Prevention.: Surveillance for selected public health indicators affecting older adults—United States. MMWR Morb Mortal Wkly Rep, vol. 48, pp. 5–8 (1999)
9. Collazo, C., Santos, J., Bernal, J., Cubo, E.: Estado sobre la situación del uso y utilidades potenciales de las nuevas tecnologías para medir actividad física. Revisión sistemática de la literatura. Atención Primaria Práctica **2**(6), 100064 (2020). (in Spanish)
10. Davis, R.: Television and the older adult. J. Broadcast. **15**(2), 153–159 (1971)
11. De la Villa, M.: Programas intergeneracionales y participación social: la integración de los adultos mayores españoles y latinoamericanos en la comunidad. Universitas Psychol. **16**(1), 157–217 (2017). (in Spanish)
12. De Juanas, A., Limón, M.R., Navarro, E.: Análisis del bienestar psicológico, estado de salud percibido y calidad de vida en personas adultas mayores. Pedagogía Soc. Rev. Interuniversitaria **22**, 153–168 (2013). (in Spanish)
13. Fouts, G., Dickson, A.: Are gerontologists ignoring television? Can. Psychol. **30**(3), 568–577 (1989)
14. Ferrín, M., González, L., Meijide-Míguez, H.: Escalas de valoración funcional en el anciano. Galicia Clínica **72**(1), 1–16 (2011). (in Spanish)
15. Forster, A., Lambley, R., Young, J.B.: Is physical rehabilitation for older people in long-term care effective? Findings from a systematic review. Age Ageing **39**, 169–175 (2010)
16. Ofli, F., Kurillo, G., Obdržálek, Š, Bajcsy, R., Jimison, H., Pavel, M.: Design and evaluation of an interactive exercise coaching system for older adults: lessons learned. IEEE J. Biomed. Health Inform. **20**(1), 201–212 (2016)
17. Garber, C.E., Blissmer, B., Deschenes, M.R., Franklin, B.A., Lamonte, M.J., et al.: Quantity and quality of exercise for developing and maintaining cardiorespiratory, musculoskeletal, and neuromotor fitness in apparently healthy adults: guidance for prescribing exercise. Position Stand. Med. Sci. Sports Exerc. **43**(7), 1334–1359 (2011)
18. Heredia, J.R., Isidro, F., Chulivi, I., Costa, M.R., Soro, J.: Determinación de la Carga de Entrenamiento para la Mejora de la Fuerza orientada a la Salud (Fitness Muscular). EF Deportes **27**(1), 1–24 (2007). (in Spanish)
19. Kubey, R.: Television and aging: past, present and future. Gerontologist **20**(1), 16–35 (1980)
20. Lesende, I.: Escalas y pruebas de valoración funcional y cognitiva en el mayor. AMF **9**(9), 508–514 (2013). (in Spanish)
21. Madrigal, M.: La estimulación cognitiva en personas adultas mayores. Revista Cúpula 4–14 (2007). (in Spanish).

22. Organización Mundial de la Salud: Ginebra. Active Ageing: A policy Framework (2002). (in Spanish)
23. Organización Mundial de la Salud: Informe Mundial sobre el envejecimiento y la salud (OMS) (2015). (in Spanish)
24. Organización Mundial de la Salud: Estrategia mundial sobre régimen alimentario, actividad física y salud (OMS) (2020). (in Spanish)
25. Phillips, E.M., Schneider, J.C., Mercer, G.R.: Motivating elders to initiate and maintain exercise. Arch. Phys. Med. Rehabil. **85**, 52–57 (2004)
26. Podsiadlo, D., Richardson, S.: The timed «Up & Go»: a test of basic functional mobility for frail elderly persons. J. Am. Geriatr. Soc. **39**(2), 142–148 (1991)
27. Riebe, D.: Exercise prescription. In: Whaley, M. (ed.) ACSM's Guidelines for Exercise Testing and Prescription, 9th edn., pp. 161–190. Lippincott Williams & Wilkins, Philadelphia (2014)
28. Rosado, M., Abásolo, M.J., Silva, T.: ICT oriented to the elderly and their active aging: a systematic review. In: Abásolo, M.J., Kulesza, R., Pina Amargós, J.D. (eds.) jAUTI 2019. CCIS, vol. 1202, pp. 134–155. Springer, Cham (2020). https://doi.org/10.1007/978-3-030-56574-9_9
29. Rosado, M., Abásolo, M.J., Silva, T.: Contenidos interactivos para TVDI destinados a reducir las alteraciones de la marcha en adultos mayores. In: IX Jornadas de Aplicaciones y Usabilidad de la Televisión Digital Interactiva-jAUTI 2020 (2020). (in Spanish)
30. Rubin, A., Rubin, R.: Older person's TV viewing patterns and motivations. Commun. Res. **9**, 287–313 (1982)
31. Ser Quijano, T., Del Peña-Casanova, J.: Evaluación Neuropsicológica y funcional de la demencia. Editores JR Prous (1994). (in Spanish)
32. Tinetti, M.E.: Preventing falls in elderly persons. J Am Geriatr Soc. **34**, 116–119 (1986)
33. Vallejo, N., Ferrer, R., Jimena, I., Fernández, J.: Valoración de la condición física funcional, mediante el Senior Fitness Test, de un grupo de personas mayores que realizan un programa de actividad física. Apunts. Educación física y deportes **2**(76), 22–26 (2004). (in Spanish)
34. Winter, M.C.S.: Promovendo a saude e prevenindo a dependencia: identificando indicadores de fragilidade em idosos independentes. Rev. Bras. Geriatr. Gerontol. **10**(3), 355–370 (1995). (in Portuguese)

Usability and UX Evaluations

UX Evaluation Methodology for iTV: Assessing a Natural Language Interaction System

Jorge Abreu[1](✉) ⓘ, Juliana Camargo[1] ⓘ, Rita Santos[2] ⓘ, Pedro Almeida[1] ⓘ,
Pedro Beça[1] ⓘ, and Telmo Silva[1] ⓘ

[1] DigiMedia, Department of Communication and Art, University of Aveiro,
3810-193 Aveiro, Portugal
{jfa,julianacamargo,almeida,pedrobeca,tsilva}@ua.pt
[2] DigiMedia, Águeda School of Technology and Management, University of Aveiro,
3754-909 Aveiro, Portugal
rita.santos@ua.pt

Abstract. The user experience can be evaluated in different ways, from a combination of approaches and techniques capable of collecting insights about a particular product or system. In the TV ecosystem research field, verifying how users react to new features is an essential step to the integration of functionalities able to enhance the user experience. This is the case of systems based on interaction by natural language (NLI), which have the potential to allow for more simplified navigation (based on conversational dynamics). However, although the spoken interactions are relevant to optimize the consumption of television content, it is essential to identify how they are received and understood by the user. In this context, this empirical study sought to analyze the experience of using an NLI system controlled by a mobile application. The evaluation was performed employing an open methodology that considers instrumental and non-instrumental qualities of the application, as well as emotional dimensions. This approach was specifically developed for UX analysis of systems and applications related to the TV ecosystem, having recorded positive results in previous studies. In the study here presented, the methodology revealed again to be suitable as it was possible to identify failures and opportunities to improve the assessed NLI system and, finally, to verify that the voice interaction system allowed users a more optimized and accessible experience.

Keywords: User Experience · Evaluation · Triangulation · Methodology · iTV · NLI system · Voice interaction

1 Introduction

Evaluating the user experience (UX) is an increasingly relevant task, often reflected in academic studies, [1], being one of the main reasons for that the set of results that a well-structured analysis can offer.

This evaluation goes beyond the observation of the responses of individuals to the anticipated use of a product, system or service [2]. With a suited methodology, it is

© Springer Nature Switzerland AG 2021
M. J. Abásolo et al. (Eds.): jAUTI 2020, CCIS 1433, pp. 149–161, 2021.
https://doi.org/10.1007/978-3-030-81996-5_11

possible to detect emotional and hedonic characteristics, such as aesthetics, stimulation and identification, which are extremely relevant in the interactions between humans and systems [3].

Therefore, an adequate UX evaluation should not be limited to the usability dimension, that is, to the evaluation of operational tasks when using a product or service. For being a global experience, it also needs to be evaluated globally, using a methodology capable of identifying all aspects involved in the user's journey. Examining this path in detail is a multidisciplinary activity, encompassing cognitive sciences, psychology, engineering and design [2].

In the interactive television (iTV) field, the central theme of this study, UX evaluations are extremely important to validate new features and improve technologies. This is the case, for example, of natural language interaction (NLI) systems to operate an iTV solution. Although it is possible to use voice assistants to perform actions on TV, the true potential of spoken interactions is not yet widely explored in this context. That is, instead of enabling conversational dynamics (the main purpose of this type of system), interactions have been limited to using voice commands to swap channels or increase volume, for example. This scenario makes UX assessments important tools for making technical advances capable of turning the interaction more user-friendly and anthropomorphic. These are two characteristics considered important for a satisfactory UX [4].

In this sense, the present study is dedicated to describing an open UX evaluation methodology for the iTV domain, how it was applied to assess an NLI system specifically designed for an iTV commercial platform, and the correspondent results. This evaluation approach, already used in previous studies [5–7] performed by the Social iTV research group (http://socialitv.web.ua.pt), is based on a triangulation of free questionnaires combined with a semi-structured interview, being adaptable to a range of applications belonging to the field of the TV ecosystem. The methodology was specified by the authors to evaluate the perspectives of users on the instrumental and non-instrumental qualities of the application, as well as the emotional reactions aroused by the episodic/cumulative UX [8].

To present the context and gathered indicators, this paper is structured as follows: Sect. 2 presents a set of instruments used to evaluate UX systems focused on human-computer interaction, unfolding to describe the approach used in the present study; the prototype of the NLI system is presented in Sect. 3; Sect. 4 details the procedures, sample, and results obtained; discussion of the results is held in Sect. 5; and finally, the conclusions are presented in Sect. 6.

2   UX Evaluation methodologies for iTV Applications

2.1   Overview

Although there is no single definition about UX, the ISO9241-110: 2010 (clause 2.15) classifies the concept as "a person's perceptions and responses as a result of the early use and/or use of a product, system, or service" [9].

UX evaluation tends to be complex as it examines different aspects arising from the use of a product or software [10] and, consequently, there is no single formula applicable to all scopes.

The dimensions to be evaluated vary according to each case or test area, as they must be appropriate and relevant to the contexts in which they are applied. In order to evaluate the UX, evaluators have at their disposal a range of methods, approaches and scales, tested and recognized over the years [2]. As the UX is by its nature a complex matter, involving various aspects and requiring different types of responses [2], its evaluation is not limited to the usability and performance of interactive solutions, covering also non-instrumental qualities such as aesthetics, stimulation, and identification; emotional reactions, such as, pleasure, attraction and control; and timeless practice [17, 19].

An analysis of UX evaluations studies related with iTV applications allowed to identify that the following free established methods have been regularly used:

1. Self-Assessment Manikin (SAM): a non-verbal pictorial assessment method that assesses levels of satisfaction, motivation and control.
2. AttrakDiff: a questionnaire based on a semantic differential scale that evaluates two components of an interactive application or product – Pragmatic and Hedonic Quality.
3. SUXES: an evaluation method for collecting subjective metrics with user experiments. It captures the expectations and experiences of individuals, making it possible to analyze the state of the application and its methods of interaction.

As the usability of the iTV applications may have an impact on the perceived non-instrumental dimensions of the UX, it is also frequent to resort to the combined use of the System Usability Scale (SUS) - a set of ten simple questions, answered by means of a five-point Likert scale, related to the overall usability of the application.

The following studies sought to evaluate the UX of products and solutions that enable human-computer interaction, most of which belonging to the context of iTV. Almost all the articles mentioned here have used more than one instrument to evaluate the user experience.

For example, Lee et al. [11] used the SAM scale combined with a semantic differential questionnaire to analyze the felling and the perceived quality of the interactive features embedded in the television.

Similar procedures were performed by Ludwig et al. [12], Rodrigues et al. [13] and Pailleur et al. [14] identifying emotional aspects related to intelligent systems from the combination of more than one instrument, such as the SAM questionnaire and semi-structured interviews.

An example of applying the AttrakDiff scale can be seen in [15], which sought to identify, among the elderly, pragmatic, hedonic and attractive components in the use of three different TV remote controls: a prototype designed especially for the elderly, the Tekpal model, aimed at senior citizens, and a traditional model, commonly used in a daily basis. The evaluation made it possible to identify the most appropriate remote control for the target users. Contrary to most of the other studies, here only the AttrakDiff was used to evaluate the user experience.

The SUXES evaluation method, in turn, was used by Turunen [16] to evaluate the UX of various modes of interaction of a home entertainment system controlled by a mobile phone. Such a method was able to collect expectations and experiences, making it possible to analyze the state of the application and its interaction methods (and compare results). The researchers combined the SUXES method with questionnaires applied before and after the test, where they requested an overall assessment of the user experience [16].

Some researchers, such as Ouyang et al. [18], used SUS as one of the methods of the UX evaluation described in the study. In this case, the authors evaluated UX in three stages. In a first moment: the participants were asked to complete a basic questionnaire about their background and daily TV use. Second, a think-aloud demonstration was presented to participants before they attempted to complete the assigned tasks. Third, participants were asked to complete the SUS questionnaire [18].

Given some of the gaps found, such as lack of clarity regarding the dimensions that were evaluated by the researchers and the use of a dominant method, a more comprehensive methodology was proposed by the Social iTV research group of the University of Aveiro (described in the following section).

2.2   Evaluation Methodology Proposal

The methodology used in this study to evaluate the experience associated with the natural language interaction with the TV set draw on the dimensions identified on a literature review oriented to the TV ecosystem, conducted by Bernhaupt and Pirker [3]. These dimensions are: i) stimulation (describes the extent to which a product can meet the user's needs with attractive functions, interactions, and content); ii) identification (a product's ability to allow a user to identify with it); iii) emotional (feelings and emotions triggered by the experience, with emphasis on satisfaction, motivation, and control); and iv) visual/aesthetic (levels of experience attractiveness). The proposal follows the CUE (Components of User Experience) model [20], which reinforces the importance of considering emotions and perceptions of instrumental qualities in articulation with the ones resulting from non-instrumental qualities.

This structure was the starting point for the development, by Abreu, Almeida, and Silva [5], of an open methodology based on the triangulation of UX instruments capable of evaluating precisely the dimensions highlighted by Bernhaupt and Pirker [3]. With this free and open methodology, the non-instrumental dimensions of stimulation and identification are evaluated using the Hedonic Quality components of the AttrakDiff questionnaire (HQ-S and HQ-I); the emotional reactions (satisfaction, motivation, and control) rely on the SAM questionnaire, whereas the visual/aesthetic dimension is obtained by the attractiveness value of the AttrakDiff (ATT). To weigh the instrumental qualities (which can give relevant insights on how the perception of usability of the application relates to its UX), the methodology proposed by the team is supported on the SUS scale and on the pragmatic dimension of the Attrakdiff questionnaire. Finally, but no less important, to complement the data obtained a semi-structured interview is carried with each of the participants who tested the system (Fig. 1).

The evaluation process is divided into three stages, the first being the preparation (which comprises the definition of objectives, the preparation of the setup, the definition of variables and the preparation of the instruments). Then, after the episodic/cumulative experience, the application of the data collection tools take place (in the order of SAM, SUS, Attrakdiff questionnaires complemented by the interview). Finally, the data collected is analyzed so that the conclusions can be addressed.

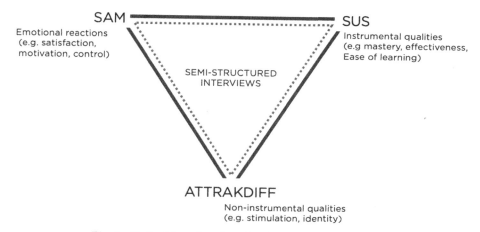

Fig. 1. Methodology based on the triangulation of UX scales.

This methodology was used in previous studies, having contributed significantly to evaluate experiences resulting from the use of: i) a mobile application centered on the recognition of audio and video of a set of interactive systems related to real-time TV services [5]; ii) an application (second screen type) aimed at the search for television content [6]; and iii) an advanced TV content aggregation User Interface that allows to offer TV and OTT contents at the same level [7]. These studies obtained consistent results, allowing to know the overall UX in relation to the evaluated systems and reinforcing the validity of the used methodology.

In the current evaluation, the authors sought to evaluate the referred dimensions related to the UX of a NLI system used in the TV context, with the aim of identify failures, correct, and add significant improvements.

3 Prototype of a Natural Language Interaction System for iTV

A voice interaction system, specifically developed for the Portuguese television context, was integrated into the main IPTV service provider in Portugal. Due to technical reasons, it was decided to upgrade an existing mobile application available to the company's customers, that worked as a virtual remote control, with a specific area integrating the NLI feature.

The interaction process starts when the user presses and hold a button (identified with a microphone icon – see Fig. 2) to utter the desired action using natural language. The captured audio is converted to text by a cloud-based Automatic Speech Recognition system (ASR), which processes and sends the spoken phrase to the iTV Set-Top Box (STB). The interface was designed to offer a fluid, natural and clear experience, including strategic resources, such as icons and phrases capable of guiding the user [16].

The user speaks and its utterance is immediately displayed in the iTV User Interface (UI), followed by a message on the TV screen indicating the correspondent intent (e.g., Searching for comedy movies). The results are presented below the message accompanied by the corresponding thumbnails. If there is a misunderstanding of

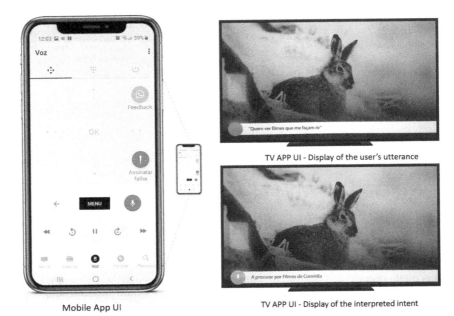

Mobile App UI

TV APP UI - Display of the user's utterance

TV APP UI - Display of the interpreted intent

Fig. 2. App UI (left) and TV app UI when searching for comedy movies (right).

the utterance by the NLU, two possible actions may occur: either the system performs an action that is not as expected or issues a decoy, such as "Sorry, I still can't help you with what you asked for".

In addition, to make the UX more contextualized [7], the user is also able to immediately report eventual errors through the mobile app, using the "flag failure" (red) button, or interact through the "feedback" (green) button, that starts a conversation on WhatsApp (with a member of the research team) enabling the user to address issues raised by its momentary UX [5].

4   UX Evaluation Process

The UX evaluation of the NLI system was carried out in a real context of use, in a Field Trial (FT), building on the potential advantages of revealing problems that would not appear in a laboratory and providing a more realistic perspective of the commonly used phrases [19]. Its main objective was to verify the viability of the solution and to analyze improvements to be made to enhance its UX.

As proposed by the team's previous work [5], the scales used (SUS [21] and AttrakDiff) were a version translated to Portuguese and made available, along with the SAM scale, in a single (online) questionnaire for the participants.

After that, the data collected by these instruments used in the evaluation was complemented by a semi-structured interview, which had as objectives: i) to collect the opinion of the participants regarding the functionalities of the NLI system; ii) to identify the possible actions to be taken to improve the overall solution, and iii) to understand the level of willingness of participants in using the solution.

4.1 Procedures

The field tests were performed by 20 users between October 2019 and April 2020, spanning in a total of 169 days. Participants used the application in their homes for daily TV consumption activities. In addition, they were encouraged to test specific functionalities through challenges (with pre-defined themes, such as asking to see comedy films, finding content of actors and actresses, increasing or lowering the volume and finding programs using similar names, among others) sent on a weekly basis by e-mail. Such autonomy given to users made it possible to assess, in a more reliable way, the experience of using the proposed solution.

After the system testing period, the UX evaluation was carried out, being this a fundamental procedure for the validation of the prototype. Users were asked to answer the online questionnaire - built from the triangulation of scales (SAM, SUS, and AttrakDiff). The questionnaire sent to the participants had the aim of identifying the following global aspects: emotions triggered using the application, usability of the natural language interaction system, specific opinions about the natural language interaction system and suggested improvements.

Then, among the 20 selected participants, the 11 most active participants were invited to participate in a semi-structured videocall interview to identify and clarify aspects relevant to the study. Some examples of questions that were asked to the participants were: "would you use the system on a daily basis?"; "what were the main problems encountered?"; "what do you believe can be improved in the application?"; and "would you use the app in place of the remote control?". This step was decisive to the evaluators, enable them to gather more consolidated opinions about the topics considered relevant for the UX evaluation.

4.2 Sample Characterization

A non-probability, by convenience, sampling was used and the prior knowledge of iTV apps was considered an inclusion criterion. Among the 20 selected participants, 75% (15) were men and 25% (5) women, with an average age of 44 years. Regarding the level of education, 45% (9) have a degree, 50% (10) a master's degree and 5% (1) a doctorate.

Among the devices, regular TVs (connected to STB) are used on a daily basis by 90% (18) of the participants, followed by Smart TVs (5–25%), applications to control the TV (5–25%), Media Players (2 -10%) and vi assistant (2–10%).

The average consumption of television was 1 h and 37 min a day. Regarding the daily frequency of use of the TV features, 50% (10) use automatic recordings, 40% (8) pause television content, 15% (3) resort to recording content, 10% (2) to TV-guide and 5% (1) to TV content search. Regarding the use of voice interaction devices, only 25% (5) stated that they had already tested or had done it daily. The assistants that appeared in the responses were Google Home, Android Auto, Google Assistant and Smart TVs with integrated voice interaction.

Then, an analysis of the volume of interactions generated by the 20 individuals belonging to the sample was performed. From this group, we chose the 11 most active for semi-structured interviews, considering the quality and frequency of interaction performed during the period that covered the tests.

4.3 Results

The SUS scale identified data on instrumental qualities, namely on efficiency, effectiveness and ease of learning of the NLI system. The prototype obtained a score of 82 (on a scale from 0 to 100), which indicates that the average value of the participants' subjective perceptions about their usability is considered "Good" (Fig. 3.) The fact that the prototype underwent a process of continuous improvement throughout the tests contributed to this positive score.

Faced with a 5-level Likert scale (SUS scale), in which 1 – "I totally disagree" and 5 – "I totally agree", the results showed that participants would like to use the NLI system frequently (a = 4.3), found it easy to use (a = 4.1), consider that its functionalities were well integrated (a = 3.9) and quickly learned how to use it (a = 4.3). These indicators corroborate the opinions collected in the semi-structured interviews. Among the 11 respondents, eight said they would use the system daily and three would adopt it for activities that require greater cognitive load, such as searching for specific content.

Regarding privacy and security, the average stood at 4.1, suggesting that participants did not feel significant concerns about these themes. In the interviews, five persons stated that the use of the application can raise privacy issues for the target public, such as undue access to users' data, although this is not a problem that directly affects them. Five participants said that the NLI-system does not generate controversies about privacy. Only one showed insecure in relation to this theme, saying that "*I have a concern for systems that are always listening to us. There must be clarity in the policy for accessing customer data*".

The less positive score was recorded in the phrase "I think that this product had many inconsistencies", a clear reflection of some failures that were found during the use of the system (for example, the request "*turnoff the (set-top) box*" was not working, and the request "*forward*" was changing to the next channel instead of forwarding the content).

When comparing the results of participants with previous experience (n = 5) and without previous experience (n = 15) in using voice interaction systems/devices, it was verified that the prototype score was slightly higher among participants with previous experience (85 out of 100). However, the prototype obtained a score of 81 by the participants without such experience, which reveals that prototype commands are probably intuitive.

Regarding the SAM scale, it was found that, on average, the parameters "satisfaction" (3.85), "motivation" (3.65) and "control" (3.5) presented a positive score (in a scale of 1 to 5) but there is still room for improvement in terms of user-system interaction. In the semi-structured interviews, the 11 participants reported that they had some kind of problem during the experiment, and the major complaints were related to ambiguous commands and the system's difficulties in perceiving commands in English (both failures/difficulties mentioned four times). Another feature that troubled users was the need to hold the phone button to activate all voice commands (problem mentioned by three participants). Two

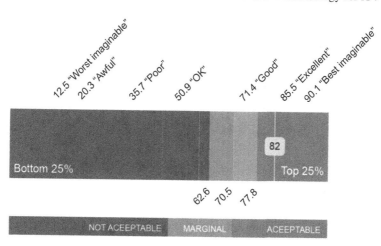

Fig. 3. Overall SUS Scale result.

of them claimed to be uncomfortable holding the button while saying the entire sentence and one reported that he had difficulties noticing when it was the exact time to release it. Although they were mentioned, these problems were not considered serious by the users interviewed, which was also reflected in the results of the questionnaires.

The "motivation" factor confirmed some desire to use the system. However, such a willingness to use the system may not be sufficient to replace the traditional remote control. The results of the semi-structured interviews showed that of the 11 participants, two stated that they would adopt the application only in conjunction with the remote control, because they consider that some tasks are easier to perform with it. One of the participants stated that it would adopt only if the app had a more practical access, because he felt uncomfortable with having to use it via the smartphone.

In view of an analysis and comparison of the data collected from the participants with (n = 5) and without previous experience (n = 15) of use voice interaction systems/devices, the results showed that in the parameters of satisfaction and motivation the scores were higher in the participants without previous experience, which may indicate that the "novelty factor" had important implications in these collected results.

Regarding the control parameter, the results showed that the participants with previous experience gave a higher score (4.00), compared to the participants without previous experience (3,33). This indicates that having a general and prior understanding of the capabilities and functionalities of voice assistants can improve and ease the experience of interaction between user-NLI system.

Regarding the AttrakDiff scale (−3 to 3), the pragmatic quality presented the lowest classification (1.05), and the aesthetic attractiveness presented the best classification (1.91). The hedonic qualities of identification and stimulation presented classifications of 1.24 and 1.56, respectively.

As for the pairs of adjectives, the pleasant-negligible and low cost-premium pairs presented negative classifications, with impact on both the pragmatic dimension and the identification dimension, which may indicate critical characteristics that should be improved. According to the results of the qualities, hedonic and pragmatic, the prototype was positioned between the "Self-oriented" and "Desired" quadrants (Fig. 4).

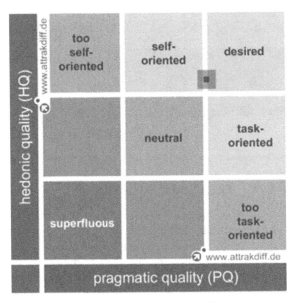

Fig. 4. AttrakDiff scale results.

In the comparison between participants with previous experience (n = 5) and those without experience (n = 15), it was found that participants with previous experience attributed higher classifications in the parameters of stimulation (1.91) and attractiveness (2,20), while the participants without previous experience attributed a higher score in pragmatic quality (1,18).

Regarding the hedonic quality of identification, both gave the same score (1,23). Within these parameters, the attractiveness obtained better scores in both groups.

The global result of the AttrakDiff scale is in accordance with the opinions of the semi-structured interviews, in which the participants stated that they would like to use the system, mainly because it simplifies the experience of television consumption.

5   Discussion

In the triangulation of the three scales (Figs. 5 and 6), it is possible to realize that the prototype is overall satisfactory in terms of UX.

Instrumental Qualities		Non-instrumental Qualities		Emotional Impact			
SUS (0 to 100)	**AttrakDiff** (-3 to 3)			**SAM** (1 to 5)			**AttrakDiff** (-3 to 3)
	PQ	HQ-S	HQ-I	Sat.	Mot.	Cont.	ATT
82	1,05	1,56	1,24	3,85	3,65	3,50	1,91
UX Dimensions	Stimulation	Indentification		Emotion			Aesthetics

Fig. 5. Global scores of field tests - triangulation of SUS, SAM and AttrakDiff.

normalized values at 100%	SUS	Attrakdiff			SAM			AttrakDiff
		PQ	HQ-S	HQ-I	Sat.	Mot.	Cont.	ATT
	82%	68%	76%	71%	71%	66%	63%	82%

Fig. 6. Normalized scores of field tests.

In relation to the instrumental qualities of the prototype, the scores on the Pragmatic Quality of the AttrakDiff scale and that of the SUS scale reflect the user's comfort in relation to the use of the product (according to the evaluation scale, the average usability value considered good is 72.40 points). However, although the obtained value (82) is a good score, it indicates that there is still room for improvement, corroborating the opinions collected in the semi-structured interviews. Individual conversations with participants allowed us to detect a set of 11 improvements, such as "finer searches", "zapping (channel surfing) like that performed by the remote control", "direct access to content already seen" and "implementation of the view command from the beginning".

The less positive score in SUS was recorded in the phrase "I think that this product had many inconsistencies", which may have influenced the "control" dimension of the SAM scale, which obtained the lowest mean (3.50) compared to the other two emotional reactions: satisfaction and motivation. On the other hand, the fact that both obtained more positive scores indicates that there was a positive affective relationship regarding the use of the prototype, which was also identified with the result of the attractiveness value of the Attrakdiff scale (ATT).

Summing up, the positive feeling regarding usability may have contributed to increase the levels of satisfaction, motivation and stimulation. On the other hand, the flaws found throughout the FT probably interfered with important aspects such as control and simplicity.

Based on these results, it can be verified, therefore, that the applied methodology allowed to evaluate all aspects considered important for the television ecosystem and helped to improve the system for the next steps, making it more robust.

6   Conclusion

The iTV ecosystem is leaning towards the increasing use of voice interaction features [22], since spoken interactions have the potential to ensure a more user-friendly and practical UX [23]. Therefore, based on this scenario, we sought to perform a thorough evaluation of the experience of using a prototype that allows natural voice interaction, from a mobile application. The main objective was to make effective contributions to the TV ecosystem, testing, once again, an approach capable of identifying relevant failures and improvements.

Using an open methodology centered on the triangulation of UX scales and complemented with interviews, it was possible to evaluate the perspectives of users on the instrumental and non-instrumental qualities of the prototype, as well as the emotional reactions triggered by its UX.

The quantitative data supported the user satisfaction, especially in relation to fundamental aspects/dimensions for the television context, such as innovation, aesthetics, comfort and intention of use (following this experimental phase). Semi-structured interviews allowed to qualitatively assess the main obstacles and positive aspects of the experience of using the proposed solution.

From the methodology adopted it was possible to identify real problems arising from the experience of using the system. In addition, the adopted methodology provided essential insights to support the idea that natural voice interaction can be well accepted by TV users.

After the evaluation cycle it was possible to move towards a more stable and complete version of the presented solution. And, in this sense, the fact that the results were obtained from the actual use of the developed prototype contributed to reaffirm the relevance of the methodology to future projects carried out within the TV ecosystem.

Finally, it is also important to highlight some limitations of the study that may have interfered with the results obtained, such as sample size, gender disparity and lack of people without high academic training.

References

1. Lallemand, C., Koenig, V.: Measuring the contextual dimension of user experience: development of the user experience context scale (UXCS). In: ACM International Conference Proceeding Series (2020)
2. Pettersson, I., Lachner, F., Frison, A., Riener, A., Butz, A.: A bermuda triangle? - A review of method application and triangulation in user experience evaluation. In: Conference on Human Factors in Computing Systems – Proceedings (2018)
3. Bernhaupt, R., Pirker, M.: Evaluating user experience for interactive television: towards the development of a domain-specific user experience questionnaire. In: Kotzé, P., Marsden, G., Lindgaard, G., Wesson, J., Winckler, M. (eds.) INTERACT 2013. LNCS, vol. 8118, pp. 642–659. Springer, Heidelberg (2013). https://doi.org/10.1007/978-3-642-40480-1_45
4. Bahlenberg, R., Yan, X.: Anthropomorphic design and anticipated user experience. In: Frontiers in Psychology (2019)
5. Abreu, J., Almeida, P., Silva, T.: A UX evaluation approach for second-screen applications. In: Abásolo, M.J., Perales, F.J., Bibiloni, A. (eds.) jAUTI/CTVDI -2015. CCIS, vol. 605, pp. 105–120. Springer, Cham (2016). https://doi.org/10.1007/978-3-319-38907-3_9
6. Ferraz de Abreu, J., Almeida, P., Beça, P.: InApp questions – An approach for contextual evaluation of applications. In: Abásolo, M.J., Almeida, P., Pina Amargós, J. (eds.) jAUTI 2016. CCIS, vol. 689, pp. 163–175. Springer, Cham (2017). https://doi.org/10.1007/978-3-319-63321-3_12

7. Velhinho, A., Fernandes, S., Abreu, J., Almeida, P., Silva, T.: Field trial of a new iTV approach: the potential of its UX among younger audiences. In: Abásolo, M.J., Silva, T., González, N.D. (eds.) jAUTI 2018. CCIS, vol. 1004, pp. 131–147. Springer, Cham (2019). https://doi.org/10.1007/978-3-030-23862-9_10
8. Roto, V., Law, E., Vermeeren, A., Hoonhout, J.: User experience white paper - Bringing clarity to the concept of user experience. In: Outcome of the Dagstuhl Seminar on Demarcating User Experience, Germany. Seminar (2011)
9. ISO 9241-210.: Ergonomics of Human-System Interaction – Part 210: Human-centered Design for Interactive Systems (formerly known as 13407). International Standardization Organization (ISO), Switzerland (2010)
10. Law, E.: The measurability and predictability of user experience. In: Proceedings of the 2011 SIGCHI Symposium on Engineering Interactive Computing Systems. EICS 2011 (2011)
11. Lee, S., Yun, M.: Interactive TV user experience in behavioral situations. In: Multi Conference on Computer Science and Information Systems, MCCSIS 2019 - Proceedings of the International Conferences on Interfaces and Human Computer Interaction 2019, Game and Entertainment Technologies 2019 and Computer Graphics, Visualization, Comp (2019)
12. Ludwig, R., Bachmann, A., Buchholz, S., Ganser, K., Glänzer, D., Matarage, A.: How to measure UX and usability in today's connected vehicles. In: Ahram, T., Taiar, R., Langlois, K., Choplin, A. (eds.) IHIET 2020. AISC, vol. 1253, pp. 17–21. Springer, Cham (2021). https://doi.org/10.1007/978-3-030-55307-4_3
13. Rodrigues, A., Machado, B., Almeida, M., Abreu, J., Tavares, T.: Evaluation methodologies of assistive technology interaction devices: a participatory mapping in Portugal based on community-based research. In: IHC 2019 - Proceedings of the 18th Brazilian Symposium on Human Factors in Computing Systems (2019)
14. Le Pailleur, F., Huang, B., Léger, P.-M., Sénécal, S.: A new approach to measure user experience with voice-controlled intelligent assistants: a pilot study. In: Kurosu, M. (ed.) HCII 2020. LNCS, vol. 12182, pp. 197–208. Springer, Cham (2020). https://doi.org/10.1007/978-3-030-49062-1_13
15. Mehrotra, S.: Potmote: a TV remote control for older adults. In: ASSETS 2018 - Proceedings of the 20th International ACM SIGACCESS Conference on Computers and Accessibility (2018)
16. Turunen, M.: User expectations and user experience with different modalities in a mobile phone controlled home entertainment system. In: ACM International Conference Proceeding Series (2009)
17. Guerino, G., Valentim, N.: Usability and user experience evaluation of natural user interfaces: a systematic mapping study. In: IET Software (2020)
18. Ouyang, X., Zhou, J.: How to help older adults move the focus on a smart TV? Exploring the effects of arrow hints and element size consistency. Int. J. Hum. Comput. Interact. 35, 1420 (2019)
19. Hassenzahl, M.: The Thing and I:Understanding the Relationship between User and Product in Funology: From Usability to Enjoyment (2003)
20. Thüring, M., Mahlke, S.: Usability, aesthetics and emotions in human-technology interaction. Int. J. Psychol. 42, 253 (2007)
21. Martins, A., Rosa, A., Queirós, A., Silva, A., Rocha, N.: European Portuguese validation of the system usability scale (SUS). Procedia Comput. Sci. 67, 293 (2015)
22. Silva, T., Almeida, P., Abreu, J., Oliveira, E.: Interaction paradigms on iTV: a survey towards the future of television. In: 9th International Multi-Conference on Complexity, Informatics and Cybernetics. IMCIC, pp. 18–23 (2018)
23. Kocaballi, A., Laranjo, L., Coiera, E.: Understanding and measuring user experience in conversational interfaces. Interact. Comput. 31, 192–207 (2019)

Evaluation of Interaction Interfaces - A Tool Proposal for Digital TV Based on Industry Standards

Raoni Kulesza(✉), Rafael Toscano, Richelieu R. Costa, Jaqueline D. Noleto, Gabriel A. Moreira, Francisco P. A. de Medeiros, and Carlos E. S. Dias

Digital Video Applications Lab – LAVID, Federal University of Paraiba, João Pessoa, Brazil
`raoni@lavid.ufpb.br`

Abstract. This work presents the specification of a testing tool according to interaction design standards and heuristics of Digital TV reception platforms, such as terrestrial and / or satellite TV receivers, integrated or not with IP networks (such as, for example, the standard 10-foot-UI). The proposed solution has two main modules. The first is represented by a Web application used for the management of users and resources (devices, metrics, tests and reports), where it is possible to use 19 categories of evaluation metrics that can be managed (edited or expanded) associated for an evaluation (test) of a given product or family of products registered in this module. The second is a mobile application that uses a navigation strategy with wizards, allowing it to conduct the tester in each of the stages of the execution of a product evaluation, as well as the generation and analysis of reports.

Keywords: DTV · 10-foot-ui · Human-computer interaction · User interface evaluation

1 Introduction

The consumption of audiovisual content has become an increasingly complex activity as new interaction interfaces, sharing, increased computational power and different modes of fruition become popular. Looking at the new tools of distribution, such as Netflix, Amazon Prime, Apple TV, Disney+, broadcasters like BBC, ABC, CBS, CNN, Globo Network and manufacturers such as Sony, Samsung and LG, it is made evident that those companies developed products and services that expanded the experience of "watching" video content through televisions over the last few years.

These new products and services are examples of how production, distribution and especially the reception of audiovisual content is a more complex activity today. It is necessary to consider that part of the knowledge to develop such products is a result of iterative, expensive, and confidential actions in these companies. The aforementioned technical or methodological knowledge are generally not in the public domain, published in scientific journals or even common amongst all professionals in the software and audiovisual fields. Consequently, it becomes arduous work, sometimes even a challenge,

M. J. Abásolo et al. (Eds.): jAUTI 2020, CCIS 1433, pp. 162–173, 2021.
https://doi.org/10.1007/978-3-030-81996-5_12

to organize the knowledge, competences and skills to integrate content and interfaces in audiovisual systems with a similar complexity to the current players in the market.

Previous research identified a gap in the literature in the Human-Computer Interaction (HCI) area to assist in the development of software for audiovisual systems, multimedia applications or hypermedia environments based on videos [2]. The productions identified in the literature review were supported mainly by traditional HCI methods, such as User-Centered Design. From a Media Study point of view, there has also been little progress in recent years. Most recent discussions already consider public engagement, however, without integration between audiovisual production, use of software and interaction characteristics.

This research aims to propose a tool that helps the evaluation of the quality of the audiovisual interaction interfaces from real market standards. To achieve that goal, a study of the technical reports and production guidelines of the main players and technologies in the market was made, to understand which criteria and quality attributes are used to produce such interfaces. The identified market practices were adapted in the form of success criteria to compose an evaluation tool. The evaluation by pre-established criteria is one of the most traditional HCI methods of interface inspection. Despite the existence of extremely popular practices such as Nielsen's heuristics, studies report the need to create and utilize contextual directives or criteria to assess the quality attributes of certain artifacts more precisely [3].

The upcoming sections of this work are organized in the following order: section two presents the mapping of the design patterns; section three describes the tool; and section four presents the discussions and developments of the study.

2 Design Patterns

This section presents the state of the art patterns of design for *10-foot-UI* interface types, that is, media devices graphic interfaces that are reproduced in big screens and utilized in average distances of 10 feet (about 3 m) by the users. A survey was carried out with the production reports of Amazon TV [4]; Android TV [5]; Samsung Smart TV [6]; TV OS apple [7] e LG webOS [8].

The classification of data was conducted based on three general categories: general design guides; aspect of navigation and data and command entry; recommendations for screens, exhibitions, and flows. This process was developed based on the principles of Grounded Theory [9]. In this data-centered methodological structure, it is customary to create connections between the results to help explain the scenery as a whole. Regarding the general design guides found in the manuals, we can highlight the aspects listed below.

Dimension, Screen Resolution and Safety Margin: The standard resolution recommended for *10-foot-UI* interface projects is Full HD (1920 × 1080) with 16x9 proportion. In specific cases, when the system also supports 4k video output, it is recommended to render the graphic elements in zoom mode (2×) or even (4×). Once the display window has been defined, the content must be adjusted to the safety margins. There is no exact consensus between the value chosen by the companies, yet the area of exhibition that might be unusable varies between 5% and 10% of the screen. Mostly, this safety margin presents a greater indentation on the sides.

Regarding the Use of Colors in the Interface, it is Recommended: Utilize colors with less saturation, for example, in the color palette of the design material, it is recommended to use tones from 600 to 900 for TV interfaces; the cold colors (blue, purple and gray) are more endorsed than the warm colors for interface elements; It is also recommended to utilize contrast ratios closer to 7:1 in the elements to meet the accessibility standards; it is also needed to check the compatibility between the image creation color profile and the exhibition one; Images generated in 4k in the P3 or Rec 2020 pattern may suffer losses when exhibited in the (sRGB) or Rec 709 profile of Full HD.

Typography: Regarding typography, it is recommended the use of fonts in the sans serif; for Full HD screen dimensions, it is recommended not to use values below 20 for size; apply different styles, thickness and font sizes to differentiate levels of information in the interface. The development guidelines also recommend that the styles must be tested in multiple reproduction devices and ensure that all the objects are visible from a 10 feet (3 m) distance.

Navigation Interfaces: There are many ways to design the content navigation in a *10-foot-UI* interface. We can classify them in procedural or element-oriented methods. A good navigation system must offer two strategies of navigation, and the user is responsible for using whatever suits him the best. Regarding the use of procedural methods such as D-pad or gestures (touch, swipe and click), it must be designed with a clear focus and selection route. The path from one item to another element must be clearly predictable and intuitive to the user. The element-oriented interfaces are available via pointing cursors or voice interfaces that are able to trigger any elements available in the system, both visible and not visible in the interface. To ensure the access to system resources with pointers, it is recommended the use of areas with larger selections to reduce the need of click precision. Regarding voice interfaces, it is endorsed the use of objective terms coupled up with actions. When the action is not possible directly, it is recommended to present a list of equivalences inside the system.

Focus and Selection: The navigable elements inside a *10-foot-UI* interface must be disposed of in a structure of states of focus and selection. The elements inside an interface may take on up to five visually distinct roles, being them: focused, unfocused, highlighted, selected, and deactivated. To ensure user's navigation it is recommended to: the focused elements and alternative options are clearly identified; apply, whenever possible, transitions between the states of the element; offer sound feedback to actions; delimit that the actions assigned to the X and Y axis are clear and kept consistent through the system; the movement of the focus is coherent with the direction chosen on the controller; when the user leaves a subsection, the parent selection should be in focus.

Text Input: The first point about this item is to minimize the filling of text fields as much as possible throughout the system. When necessary, the strategies that may enhance this experiences are: predict answers or common actions and offer then in the form of buttons; allow text entry via voice capture; utilize the virtual keyboard of the system itself to maintain consistency with other applications or even pairing up with secondary devices such as smartphones and tablets; use typed content recommendation system; offer preliminary search results; allow the connection of external peripheral devices and adapt the interface for this.

2.1 Metrics

From the survey carried out it was possible to organize a set of metrics and criteria for usability inspection. These criteria reflect practices recommended by companies for the development of new products. The 44 inspection criteria can be found in the table below and are divided into 19 categories (Table 1).

Table 1. Inspection criteria.

Category	Inspection criteria
Help	The graphic elements of the application must be explained
	Help instructions should preferably be offered next to the interface elements (buttons, text boxes, etc.)
Shortcuts	Shortcuts should be offered for experienced users to perform priority system tasks
Search	The interface must have search engines
Settings	The application must allow users to return to the default configuration or some previous configuration
User Control	The system should allow the user to close, minimize or maximize the application whenever he wishes
Colors	Colors must maintain RGB values within the range of 16 to 240
	Warm colors, such as red and orange, should have low intensity. Pure black and white colors should not be used
	The application must use dark text on a light background
Data Entry	The data entry fields owe their consistency throughout the system
	The application must offer recurring entries to users in order to decrease the filling time and the possibility of entering incorrect data
	The application must inform the user of the data entry format, as well as the units of the expected values
	The application must offer the ability to autocomplete data entry based on the values kept in memory
	The application must provide different selection methods, for example, selecting the elements from a list of options, as an alternative to data entry
	The validation of the input data must be performed in real time, as soon as the user enters the data

(*continued*)

Table 1. (*continued*)

Category	Inspection criteria
Feedback	The application must clearly respond to users' actions
	The application must clearly show where the user is located
	Tasks canceled in the application must stop immediately and provide appropriate feedback
	The user must be informed if a process requires a long time to run, making the user need to wait longer than usual
Focus	The user must clearly perceive when the interface objects are selected or moved
	The application must differentiate a selected option from others not selected
Icons	Icons should help users to better understand the tasks to be performed in the application
Internationalization	Interface elements, including help elements, must be offered in different languages depending on the computer configuration or user option
Margins	The size of the screen elements must be proportional to the distance between them
	The margins must have a greater indentation on the sides
Navigation	The application must maintain the consistency and coherence of the navigation on the current screen in relation to all the screens that compose it
	The information must be presented hierarchically (from general to specific, by theme, etc.)
	All screens must have an option to access the home screen
User Preference	The application should suggest content to the user based on their preferences and history of selected options
Error avoidance	The application must provide messages that are easy to understand to prevent errors
	Confirmations must be required for critical options
	Error messages must use consistent terminology and design throughout the application
	Error messages should suggest the cause of the issue
	Error messages should indicate what action the user should take to correct a problem
	Error messages that use sounds should remain consistent and be accompanied by a description of the problem

(*continued*)

Table 1. (*continued*)

Category	Inspection criteria
Security and Safety	The application must ask the user to confirm actions that have drastic, negative or destructive consequences
Simplicity	The interface elements must be clear and intuitive
Text/Labels	The texts/labels must have a minimum size of 18 points
	The texts/labels must be in a sans-serif font
	The length of the texts must not exceed 90 words on the screen or 45 words on a quarter of the screen
	The application texts must be duly observed from a distance of 3 to 5 m
Undo/Redo	Users should have the option to reverse their actions
	The application must offer the possibility to return to any previous point of use
	The application must offer options to undo and redo actions or tasks of the application

3 Evaluation Tool Proposal

From the review of the manuals and technical guidelines, success criteria were organized to compose the interface evaluation. Those criteria resulted in the business rules behind a multiplatform assessment tool. The steps considered for the inspection of the tool are: (1) registration of administrators and testers; (2) register the devices in the system; (3) clearance of the device or product for testing; (4) inspection of the product; (4) automatic report generation. The stages listed below are executed from two modules: (1) The Web module, created to help admins to register testers, devices and evaluation items; (2) The mobile module, created to help the tester in the evaluation of the products through all of its interface.

3.1 Web Module: Evaluation Management

In this module, an administrative panel allows the test administrator to manage four entities: users, devices, evaluation items and reports. Thus, the admin can register a tester, a new device, add which evaluation items should be used and finally view the report for this inspection.

The Web module has 6 main features from a home screen: 1) general system options in a drop-down menu in the upper right corner (profile, language, settings); 2) start panel with a dashboard with statistics management (users, devices and reports); 3) management of device registrations; 4) user management; 5) management of items and assessment metrics; and 6) report management. Figure 1 shows the home screen with dashboard and other 4 functionalities in the menu on the left side. Figure 2 illustrates the continuation of the dashboard screen.

Fig. 1. Web module's Dashboard - Part 1

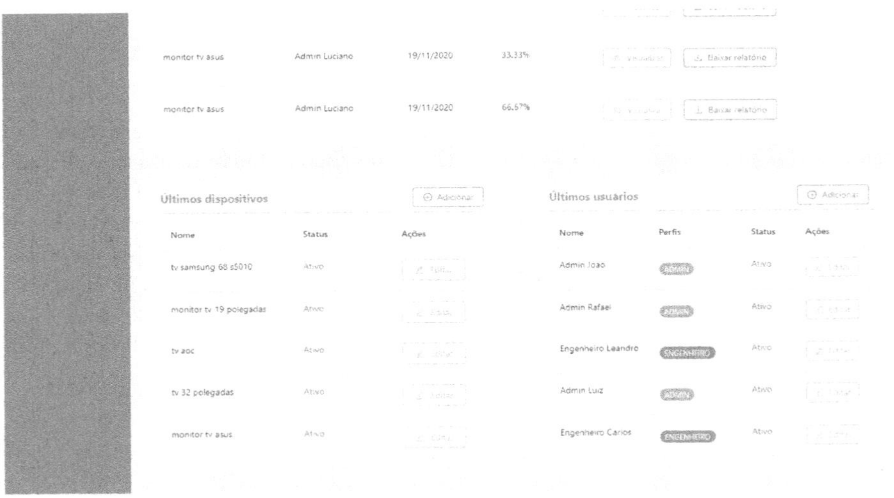

Fig. 2. Web module's Dashboard - Part 2

The management of devices and evaluation items are the most relevant functionalities of the systems. The device management allows the registration of a family of products that have a predetermined base navigation map that may be reutilized for all similar products of the same series. Figure 3 illustrates the registration screen for new devices. In it, we can see the fields that make up a device in the system, which are: 1) Name; 2) Description; 3) Status; 4) Navigation Map. All fields are editable, and the navigation map can be created with the help of the screen creation wizard, shown in Fig. 4.

Fig. 3. Web module's device management screen

Fig. 4. Wizard for creating screens and navigation map

The management of administration items allows the reuse of items and metrics of evaluation automatically once items represent a base of knowledge from the studies of the standards of the field. (with 19 categories and 44 metrics). The base of knowledge, in addition to being shared by all users, can be edited or evolved whenever necessary. Figure 5 shows the management screen for the evaluation categories and metrics. Figure 6, on the other hand, illustrates the use of a series of screens pre-registered in the system that can be associated with the evaluation items also previously registered in the evaluation categories and metrics management option.

Fig. 5. Web module's management screen for the evaluation categories and metrics.

Fig. 6. Screens wizard on devices management reusing evaluation categories and metrics.

The Web system was developed based on an N layers architecture, with the implementation using Web technologies (both in front-end and back-end) based on JavaScript (NodeJS and ReactJS) and the database used MongoDB.

3.2 Mobile Module: Execution of the Evaluation

The focus of the mobile module is the testing user. The application usage journey predicts that the user navigates through a set of facilitating screens (wizards) that helps in the verification of the registered items. Figure 7 shows (clockwise): 1) main application screen; 2) the option to choose a device for testing; 3) the navigation map for evaluating a device; 4) the evaluation run and a screen (Splash); 5) the option to view a test report for a device; 6) part of the test report for a screen (Splash).

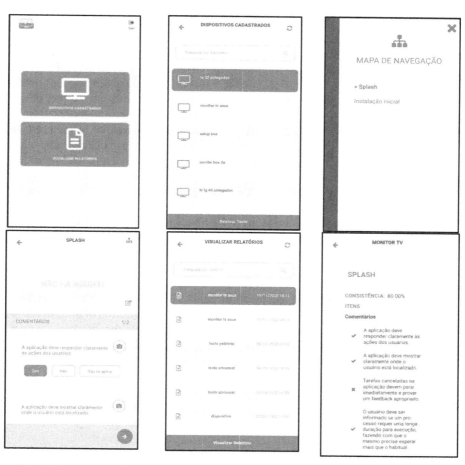

Fig. 7. Screens wizard on devices management reusing evaluation categories and metrics.

At the end of the process of navigating through the screens, fulfillment of the questionnaire, inclusion and submission of pictures and videos for verification, the tester may generate a report that can be shared or saved for posterior examination. This report evaluates items such as general consistency and details the criteria met and not met screen by screen. The mobile module facilitates the applicability in a context of specific domain tests (devices like Digital TV equipment, receptors, and media centers) without a big effort or advanced software or usability testing knowledge, a very important characteristic when the product quality assurance team are not very experts on the subject.

The architecture of the system is based on the Single Page Application (SPA) model, utilizing React Native as the technology for application development and integrating with the Web module with REST API.

4 Case Study

In order to apply the principles and the tool, a use case was done with a satellite, cable and terrestrial TV signal receiver industry. Among the company's products, there are UHF/VHF antennas, satellite dishes and satellite and terrestrial TV signal receivers. The reasoning behind this case was the absence of a test process for the digital and hybrid TVs of the company, in relation to the functionalities and the user interaction design project.

The use of testing methodologies is known to improve the quality of the products in the process of development and distribution. In the specific case of this company, it was realized that the metrics for inspection could be integrated to the functional testing cycle of the device, a process which already occurred inside the institution manually, and without consistent record keeping. The adaptation of this content resulted in the creation of four routines or test templates, being them: basic functioning, basic navigation, advanced navigation and usage quality. These routines involve everything from checking if the receiver turns on, recognizes the remote control, the user's permission to restore the factory patterns of the system and even the existence of multiple fields of interaction, such as D-Pad, voice and pointer.

The organization of the routines was done once part of the product recommendations are related to the user experience among all the audiovisual systems, that is, both hardware and software. That can be realized, for example, in the association of the criteria: (a) Functioning directional arrows of the controller; (b) Elements of the interface are completely visible on the screen; (c) Actions of the remote controller have visual feedback. Each one of these routines can be classified as mandatory, essential or complimentary, according to the objectives of the managers and applied distinctly in the testing phase. For instance, functioning tests are applied in many random devices with the objective of verifying the batch of equipment. Navigation and quality control tests, on the other hand, can be performed on a smaller scale, as software replicability is possible in the other devices.

Lastly, it was realized that the technical recommendations regarding creation could be allocated in a new inspection routine, focusing on evaluating the quality of the interfaces in order to help in the acquisition process of new products. Along with the criteria adaptation, it was found that the segmented structure of the system in managers and testers is also functional in the enterprise context since it organizes the professionals, the information and the results in a consistent manner.

5 Conclusion

This work described a tool proposal for the evaluation of audiovisual system interaction interfaces in the Digital TV domain. To this end, a mapping of *10-foot-UI* interface standards from the players in the market and an application was designed, focused on two main users, administrators and testers. The system was developed and tested internally regarding its correct functioning with automatic testing tools and concept-wise manually through the evaluation of two products of a Brazilian company. This assessment, even in its preliminary form, allowed the following conclusions: (a) the organization of hierarchy through the proposed strategies was a clear and viable approach for the final implementation of the service in sectors of quality control and product; (b) The initial challenge, from HCI, of establishing quality inspections with market standards was bypassed satisfactorily; (c) the logic of the tool and the implemented criteria can be replicated to items such basic operation ones (device turns on, recognizes signal) and accessibility. It is also perceived that the tool created during this research, even in its initial form, can benefit other domains, provided that the concept of manager and executor and item inspection is utilized in matters of security and safety, for instance. The impacts of these elements are due in future studies, in continuation of this research.

Acknowledgements. This work was partially granted by Perez-Guerrero Trust Fund for South-South Cooperation, UNITED NATIONS, INT/19/K08 *"Digital Terrestrial Television Applied to the Improvement of Developing Countries Peoples: Argentina, Brazil and Cuba"*.

References

1. Becker, V., Abreu, J., Nogueira, J., Cardoso, B.: O desenvolvimento da TV não linear e a desprogramação da grelha. Observatório (OBS*) **12**(1), 199–216 (2018)
2. Toscano, R.M., de Souza, H.B.A.M., da Silva Filho, S.G., Noleto, J.D., Becker, V.: HCI methods and practices for audiovisual systems and their potential contribution to universal design for learning: a systematic literature review. In: Antona, M., Stephanidis, C. (eds.) HCII 2019. LNCS, vol. 11572, pp. 526–541. Springer, Cham (2019). https://doi.org/10.1007/978-3-030-23560-4_38
3. Hermawati, S., Lawson, G.: Establishing usability heuristics for heuristics evaluation in a specific domain: is there a consensus? Appl. Ergon. **56**, 34–51 (2016)
4. Amazon: "Design and User Experience Guidelines I Amazon Fire TV" (2018). https://goo.gl/TEr87Q
5. Google: "Introduction - Android TV," Android Tv. https://goo.gl/Aqe3oV
6. Samsung: "Design I SAMSUNG Developers," Design your app for Samsung Smart TV (2015). https://goo.gl/vNpvWj
7. Apple: "Human Interface Guidelines" tvOS Design Themes (2018). https://goo.gl/mdbDmB
8. LG Developer I webOS TV : Design Principles (2016). https://goo.gl/xC7Wzm
9. Tarozzi, M.: O que é a grounded theory. Petrópolis - RJ: Editora Vozes (2016)

Author Index

Printed in the United States
by Baker & Taylor Publisher Services